Tea Shop Walks

in the

LAKE DISTRICT

Mary Welsh

- *25 scenic walks including traditional tea shops* •

D0954617

Dalesman

Dalesman Publishing Company
Stable Courtyard, Broughton Hall,
Skipton, North Yorkshire BD23 3AZ

First Edition 1998

Text © Mary Welsh, 1998
Illustrations © Donald Dakeyne
Maps by Jeremy Ashcroft

Cover: The Yew Tree, Seatoller, by Geoff Cowton

A British Library Cataloguing in Publication record
is available for this book

ISBN 1 85568 141 2

Printed by Midas Printing (HK) Ltd

Tea Shop Walks

in the

LAKE DISTRICT

Mary Welsh

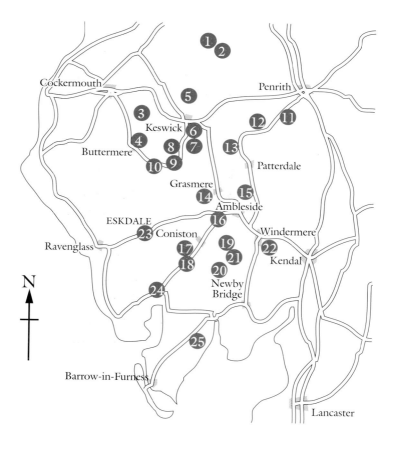

WALKS

INTRODUCTION

Each circular walk in this little book starts close to a pleasing teashop, where you can spoil yourself at the end of the day. The walks vary in length between four and eight-and-a-half miles and are designed for the 'middle-range' walker. Some keep to the valleys and others climb onto the fells. None goes onto the highest peaks.

The teashop for each walk might be a café or a small restaurant, and might serve meals into the evening or close after teatime. Opening times have been given but these may change depending upon the weather or the season. Phone numbers enable you to check.

All the teashops have been sampled – and what a pleasure this has given the writer! The food, hygiene, service and ambience were of a universally high standard and it would be fun to visit them all again.

The weather in the Lake District can be fickle and walkers should carry good waterproofs, high energy food, a drink and a map. It is wise to wear walking boots.

There is nowhere in England quite as lovely as the Lake District; take time to appreciate it, pause often, listen and look. The walks are routed along rights of way or permissive paths. As you go remember to close gates and keep dogs under close control. Take home only your photographs and memories.

For each walk the grid reference for parking has been given. For those walkers who use public transport the booklet 'Getting Around Cumbria and the Lake District' gives bus, coach, train and ferry times.

The booklet is obtained from tourist information centres or on the Internet at http://www.cumbria.gov.uk. The

INTRODUCTION

Journey Planner telephone inquiry line number is 01228 606000.

The walks were completed and checked in 1998.

Good walking!

PUBLISHER'S NOTE

The information given in this book has been provided in good faith and is intended only as a general guide. Whilst all reasonable efforts have been made to ensure that details were correct at the time of publication, the author and Dalesman Publishing Company Ltd cannot accept any responsibility for inaccuracies. It is the responsibility of individuals undertaking outdoor activities to approach the activity with caution and, especially if inexperienced, to do so under appropriate supervision. They should also carry the appropriate equipment and maps, be properly clothed and have adequate footwear. The sport described in this book is strenuous and individuals should ensure that they are suitably fit before embarking upon it.

OLD SMITHY TEAROOM

This walk takes you through quiet pastures, along narrow country lanes and beside a glorious waterfall deep in a hidden ravine.

DISTANCE: 6 miles (10km)
TIME: 3 hours
MAP: OS Pathfinder 576 OS OL 5 (new series)
TERRAIN: Easy walking. The pastures can be muddy after rain, strong walking shoes or boots advisable.
PARKING: Free car park in centre of village. GR 323398. Or beside the tearoom. GR 323397.

The Old Smithy Tearoom has tables outside overlooking Gill Beck. In January and February it opens only at weekends; in March and October to December inclusive for five days a week; and from June to September inclusive for six days. It is always closed on Tuesdays and also on Christmas Day and Boxing Day. In high summer it opens from 10am to 6pm and at other times 10.30am to 5pm. Walkers are most welcome but are asked to leave their dogs outside. All the food is homemade. Tel. 016974 78246.

The attractive fell village of Caldbeck takes its name from the Norse name for the local stream, Kald Beck, which hurries through it. Colourful cottages line the quiet streets and the tranquillity is all-pervasive. In the 18th century it was a noisier, busier place when the river provided water power for its bobbin, paper and corn mills, and miners trudged to the Caldbeck Fells for lead and copper.

Leave the car park by the entrance.

Go over the road and continue along Friars Row. Cross the delightful packhorse bridge (rebuilt in 1793) on the right to go down steps to St Mungo's well. Here converts to Christianity were baptised in the 6th century.

Beyond stands the parish church of St Kentigern (another name for St Mungo), which dates from the 12th century. Close by the church door can be seen the gravestone of John Peel, the 18th century huntsman. Nearby is the grave of Mary Harrison, known as the Beauty of Buttermere. She attracted the attention of John Hadfield and married him not knowing that he was already married. He was eventually hanged, not for bigamy but for defrauding the post office.

After visiting the church, leave the churchyard by the main gates and turn right to pass the Oddfellows Arms. John Woodcock Graves, who wrote the words of the song 'D'ye ken John Peel with his coat so grey ...', lived in a house opposite the pub and was a good friend of the huntsman.

Continue on to pass, on the left, the village toilets, behind which stand a clogmaker's shop and a forge. On the opposite side of the road, abutting the river, is the Old Smithy Tearoom.

Stroll on along the B5299. By the school, look in the wall for the Spit Stone. For over a hundred years the children of Caldbeck have spat in the stone. It is believed it once stood on the ground with vinegar in it. Money was placed in the bowl when villagers had the plague to pay for food brought in from other areas.

Go on to see the Old Map Shop, a picturesque one-up-and-one-down building, once the village school. Across the B-road stands a farmhouse named Todcrofts. Here Mary Harrison (the Beauty of Buttermere) lived after her earlier ordeal, happily married to the farmer and raising her family.

Walk up the lane behind the Old Map Shop. Cross Gill Beck, ignore the footpath on the left and take the narrow reinforced lane on the left. Beyond the last house on the right take a signposted way on the left. Ignore the arrowed stile and walk the gated hedged path just before it on your right. Stride on to a narrow road and turn left.

Stroll on with care to take the right turn for Hudscales farm. Ascend the concrete track and, at a junction of tracks, go right along a glorious green lane. Remain on this until you reach another road, where you turn left to walk into the hamlet of Nether Row.

Beyond the first house on the right, walk right to take

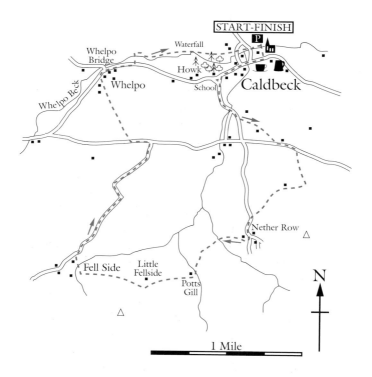

the reinforced track, signposted Potts Gill, which takes you through quiet countryside. Follow the waymarks around Potts Gill, left, right and then right again across a footbridge. Walk ahead along the continuing footpath over the fell to pass on your right Little Fellside farm.

Press on along the farm's access track, from where there are wonderful views over the rolling pastures to the hamlet of Fellside. Pass the gracious outdoor centre. At the narrow lane, turn right to walk the hedged way for three-quarters of a mile until you reach a T-junction. Turn left and, after 200 yards, take the signposted footpath on the right. Drop down the pasture to walk a hedged farm track to Whelpo.

Turn right and cross the sturdy Whelpo Bridge on your left. Beyond, go right along the permissive path. No directions are needed to follow the glorious Whelpo Beck downstream through alders and, in summer, flower carpeted dells.

The well defined path leads to the Howk, a deep ravine worn into limestone, which once had a natural stone bridge across it. Through this magnificent gorge the beck descends in great haste and by several tempestuous waterfalls to pass the old Mary Bobbin Mill, which was in use until 1924. Look for the well preserved open-sided shed, built for drying coppice wood.

Follow the path into Caldbeck. At the road, turn left to walk to a pond, set in a large un-enclosed green and known locally as Claydubs. Once it was a claypit for bricks. There is a convenient seat for enjoying this lovely corner. South-east of the pond is the exit of the car park. Hopefully you have left yourself time to enjoy your tea at the Old Smithy.

FELLSIDE TEA ROOM

C limb gently through pastures onto the quiet isolation of the Caldbeck Fells for a wonderful feeling of 'getting away from it all'.

DISTANCE: 5 miles (8km)
TIME: 3 hours
MAP: OS OL 5 (new series)
TERRAIN: Few signposts on the moor. The mine road takes you high along the side of Low Pike – dryshod and easily.
PARKING: East end of the village. GR 343386.

The diminutive Fellside Tea Room, adjoining the post office and stores, provides a splendid Back o' Skidda cream tea – if the wholemeal scones are hot you are doubly blessed. The tea room opens from 10am to 5pm, all year round, closing Sundays, Christmas Day and Boxing Day. There are outside tables for hot days, and dogs can be hitched to them. When the cafe was decorated a tiny iron fireplace was revealed. Behind the tearoom is a small kitchen and the owners believe that once it was a two-roomed cottage.

Hesket Newmarket has a fine wide street with many 18th century houses and a central Market Cross on the village green. Hesket gained the right to hold a market in 1751. It included cattle and sheep fairs. Look for the 200 year old bull ring by the Cross. In winter fell ponies seek shelter in the village from the bleak heights. Maybe as you walk through the village you will see cars setting off for a wedding; on these occasions children stretch ropes across the road, removing them only when guests throw coins as a 'fine'.

From the car park, walk left through the delightful village, with the Market Cross to your right and then Fellside Tea Room to your left. Ignore the main road as it swings right towards Caldbeck and walk a few paces along The Street, passing the Temperance Hall and then Beech Cottage. Just beyond the first left turn to Woodhall, take the steps, on your left, which lead up the slope to a signposted stile.

Continue ahead, with a fence and a stream to your left, to the next stile – most of the stiles on this walk have tall handposts, which help you to locate them. Continue steadily upwards to the next stile, which lies to the right of a metal gate and is obscured by a hawthorn bush. Go on the stiled way to pass through a gate to a track beside a wall, which leads you to the narrow access road to Hudscales farm.

Just before the farmhouse, bear left, following the sign
for the camping barn. Keep with the track as it winds
right and go through a gate onto the fell. Bear left along
the track, keeping parallel with the wall on your left. At
the wall ahead, pass through a gate, the right of two.

Beyond, head slightly right to a stile over a fence,
stretching across the moor. And then, in the same general
direction, go on to step across a narrow stream. Once
over head on to join a wide, smooth grassy trod and
walk right to a high ladderstile – over the same wall you
passed through earlier.

Step across a small stream just beyond the stile and bear
slightly left on a green trod. Stride on along the obvious
way. As you near the low spoil-heaps of earlier mining,
you have a choice, depending upon whether you want to
see the old mine, close at hand. If no, go off right
towards two derelict buildings on a wide green trod. If
yes, follow the not very clear right of way. This leads
through the tips to a small stream, crossed by a step.

Go on ahead to join a mine road and walk right. Follow
the road through more mining spoil, and continue where
it swings right. Soon it is joined, from the right, by the
green trod you might have chosen to take.

The easy mine road continues as a glorious high-level
way, with views across the Solway. Where the track
divides take the lower level and continue on to a wide
track coming up from the valley. Here turn right and
follow it down and down to the hamlet of Nether Row.

Go through a gate to pass Clay Bottom Farm and stroll
on to pass more dwellings, ignoring all left and right

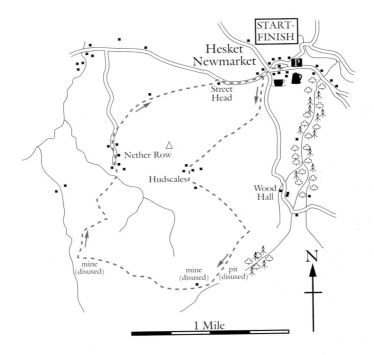

turns. Dawdle along the lane and, where it makes a gentle left turn, take the signposted footpath on the right. This is a wide hedged green lane, a joy to walk, through delightful pastures. Pass a barn and a small planting of Scots pine. Cross the access road to Hudscales to climb a stile into a pretty hedged path.

Beyond the next stile, head across the pasture towards Street Head Farm to a stile into a walled track. Once over a second stile, turn left to join The Street. Stroll right into Hesket and the start of the walk.

THE LITTLE TEAROOM

W H I N L A T T E R   F O R E S T

*A*fter climbing rides and paths through the forest, this walk takes you out onto the tops.

DISTANCE: 5 miles (8km)
TIME: 4 hours
MAP: OS OL 4
TERRAIN: Good paths through forest. Easy walking on fells – boots required. In the mist stay in the forest and do not attempt the fell tops.
PARKING: Pay-and-display car park at Whinlatter Visitor Centre, Whinlatter Pass. GR 208245.

This pleasing, elevated tearoom has fantastic views. It is open all the year round except for Christmas Day, and if bad weather has closed the Pass. Opening times: summer 10am-5pm and winter 10am-4pm. Walkers are made very welcome and you can enjoy the special 'fellwalkers' slice' with a large pot of tea. Lots of picnic tables outside and a hitching rail for dogs. Tel 017687 78068.

Whinlatter Forest Park, one of the Forest Enterprise's (formerly the Forestry Commission's) oldest forests, and England's only mountain forest, lies on the hills above Keswick. Some of the tracks and paths look alike and it is advisable to make use of the trail marker posts and junction marker posts (the latter found on the forest guide). Scattered about the forest are information boards telling you, for example, about its history, planning, landscaping, animal and bird life and how the trees are nurtured.

Leave the visitor centre and tearooms by the signpost marked

'Trails' and walk on to the next signpost, similarly labelled. Follow the posts, with red, green and blue bands, until you reach a clearing, Horsebox Crossroads, with stone benches, from where you can enjoy the fine view.

Bear left and begin climbing a narrower way, as directed by posts with single bands of green. At the forest road, turn left and follow the gently rising way as it winds round right. Where the track divides, at Tarbarrel Moss (marker post 3), take the right branch. Follow the track and keep winding left, ignoring the rough track that goes on ahead.

Enjoy the delightful terraced way as it contours around Ullister Hill, with banks of heather on either side and glorious views down towards Lorton.

Pause to look back at the dramatic tops of Grisedale Pike,

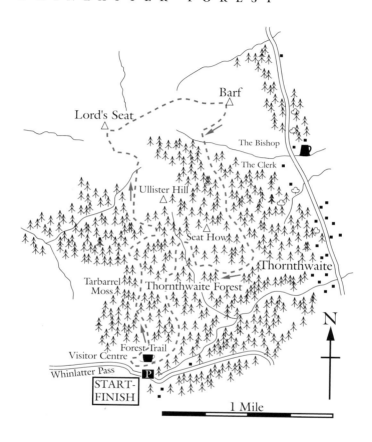

Hobcarton Crag, Hopegill Head, Whiteside and the tip of Grasmoor. Then look ahead to see the aim of the walk, Lord's Seat (1,811 ft/552m).

Follow the good path to a T-junction (post 5 and then 6), where you turn left to go on through heather and scattered young pines. Climb steadily, above the tree line, to a stile over the boundary fence (post 23). Pause here to look across the Solway to Criffel mountain. Then head on up to the bare summit. It is adorned with several old iron fence posts, all that remains of three fences that met here, and a few boulders.

Take another pause to look down on lovely Bassenthwaite Lake above which stands Ullock Pike, with Skiddaw broodingly towering above.

Two paths lead right (east) from the summit. Both soon join up and head on in the direction of Barf, a shoulder of Lord's Seat, clearly seen over a peaty depression. From the rather wet hollow it looks a steep climb, but as you begin to ascend, it is short and easy, taking you through banks of heather to the tiny summit (1,536 feet/468m). From here look down on the marsh between Bassenthwaite Lake and Derwent Water.

Leave the top by the clear path and follow it as it winds right, descending gently, with a fine view of the waterfall in Beckstones Gill. It continues to the beck, which you cross on convenient boulders. Scramble up the bank opposite to a stile into the forest once more, at post 21.

Climb a few yards to join the forest road and bear left. Ignore any other turns and go on ascending gently along the terraced way, which is bordered with ferns, mosses and foxgloves. Almost at the brow, where there are few trees, look down to the side of Barf to see a rugged whitened pinnacle, known as the Bishop of Barf. Look to the foot of the hill to see (just a speck really) another whitened rock, known as The Clerk. Both The Clerk and

The Bishop are kept white by the landlord of the Swan Hotel, which you can see in the valley bottom.

Legend has it that a Bishop of Derry and his horse are buried below The Clerk. The Bishop, while on his way to Derry by way of Whitehaven, accepted a wager in the inn to ride his horse to the top of Barf, and the whitened pinnacle marks the place where the horse stumbled and both died.

At a Y-junction continue ahead (post 8). Stride on to a T-junction, where you go right (9). Follow the track as it makes a gentle curve and, at post 10, ignore the left branch of a Y-junction. Stroll on to make another wide curve and at a division of ways (post 1) take the left branch to descend steadily to the Visitor Centre.

CROFT HOUSE CAFÉ

his is a glorious walk, with a fine shoreside path, glimpses of three lakes and a pleasing path through a secret valley and Mill Gill.

DISTANCE: 4 miles (6.5km)
TIME: 2-3 hours
MAP: OS OL 4
TERRAIN: Easy walking. Gentle climb through the secret valley. The path through Mill Gill is easy to walk when dry but take the alternative route after rain.
PARKING: Two pay-and-display car parks in Buttermere. Also parking at the café, for patrons.

Croft House Cafe is for walkers and a warm welcome awaits. There are many tables inside, with room for boots and waterproofs. Outside picnic tables face south-west and catch the afternoon sun. Here dogs can be tied. The cafe is open from Good Friday to the end of October and on all Bank holidays, from 10.30am to 5.30pm. It is closed on Saturdays. Tel 017687 70235.

Buttermere is a small village of about 50 inhabitants. It lies between Crummock Water and the lake from which it takes its name, on the only place where there is room for its cottages, farms, church, old school and hotels. From the shores of these two lovely lakes rise the steep slopes of some of the higher mountains of the Lake District. Water that overflows from Buttermere is carried by the Dubbs into Crummock Water and its excess is in turn carried by the River Cocker to the Derwent.

Leave the village by a signposted kissing gate in the car park behind

the Fish Hotel. It lies on the right side, almost at the far end, and is difficult to spot if the car park is full. Walk ahead beside the chattering Mill Beck to pass below tall trees. When in sight of Crummock Water ignore the large footbridge on the right and go on to the end of the fence on your right.

Turn left and follow a narrow path that encircles Nether How, a large, oak-covered mound, with fingers of rock stretching out into the lake. From here you can see the strip between Buttermere and Crummock Water. The two lakes were once one, the flat area formed by debris laid down after the Ice Age and stabilised by vegetation.

Once round the mound climb the stile and continue parallel with the lake to cross Mill Beck on a small footbridge. Stroll on to go through a kissing gate, over a footbridge and past a jetty. Follow the arrow directing you left through more woodland to a kissing gate to the road. Cross and climb gently to join a wide grassy trod going left. This was once the only route into Buttermere and was used by horses pulling carts.

Descend from the brow to join the road that winds round Hause Point – today's route into Buttermere. Go on for 50 yards and then bear right through a small car park. Follow the clear, grassy way, passing through gates, as it winds below Rannerdale Knotts. The path comes close to Squat Beck. Do not cross, but continue bearing right, passing through a gate on the right to begin the gentle climb through the tranquil secret valley. When Norman marauders reached this area, the defenders encouraged them to think this was the way to the

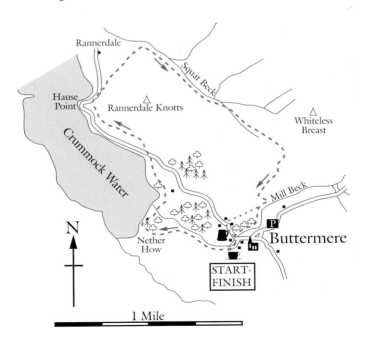

settlement so that they could be shot by archers on the heights.

As you climb pause to look back to see the lake cradled in a V-shape between two steep slopes, with Loweswater glimpsed beyond. Continue to the brow, where you will want to sit and enjoy the magnificent view of Buttermere and its surrounding heights.

Then begin your descent towards the village and lake. At a division of paths, take the left branch to walk on to a wall. Here, depending on the conditions underfoot, you should decide on your return. If it is a fine, dry day, stroll left and continue beside the wall to a large stile into Mill Gill. Turn right and follow the path through the many oaks to reach the village just above the café. If this path is unsuitable, walk right and follow the wide way as it bears steadily right to come to the road by the village's higher car park. Descend left and continue to the cross roads, where you go right to reach Croft House Cafe.

THE OLD SAWMILL

T his is an exciting climb to an arm of Skiddaw, followed by a stroll along a wide, easy-to-walk ridge.

DISTANCE: 5 miles (8km)
TIME: 3-4 hours
MAP: OS OL 4
TERRAIN: Clear tracks and paths. Some scrambling required to reach the summit of the Pike. Do not attempt in the mist.
PARKING: Forest Enterprise car park at the foot of the Dodd, and in front of the Old Sawmill tearoom. GR 235282.

Around 1890 the Mirehouse Estate was using horses to extract timber from Dodd Wood. It harnessed the power of Skill Beck and built a sawmill. In the 1970s the last log was cut and the old sawmill now serves as a delightful tearoom, with some of the original machinery and tools on display. The teashop is open every day, April to October inclusive, 10am to 5.30pm. All the food is homemade and the scones, with bilberries and cream, after a long walk, are most acceptable. Tel. 017687 74317.

Once the Dodd would have been forested with deciduous woodland. This was cleared over many years and the fell slopes left bare. Many trees were felled for use in the 1914-18 war. During the 1920s rapid replanting took place, with no thought for the appearance of the slopes. They were blanketed with serried ranks and straight-edged plantations of conifers. In the last 20 years, first the Forestry Commission, then Forest Enterprise, employed a landscape artist to design a forest with more sympathetic edges, to vary the

species and to blend the woodland into the landscape.

From the teashop, cross the A591, and walk left for 50 yards to take a signposted track on the right. Follow the hedged way as it swings right and then left as it winds through the gardens of Mirehouse, a 17th century manor house. Just before a small beck, bear left and continue to a gate.

Stroll on to visit St Bega's, a small, beautifully maintained church, which lies to the left of the path. Return along the track from the church and follow it as it skirts a delightful copse of oak. Follow this excellent track all the way to a narrow road, which you can cross to take the waymarked path over pastures to the A591. Walk right for 500 yards. Cross and take the signposted track that climbs steeply uphill to a gate onto the fell.

Climb, right, a steepish way with a fence to the left, beyond which lies a clear-felled area. Follow the path as it bears left, and still up, until the grassy fell levels out. Here a distinct path bears right and climbs upwards, zigzagging as it ascends, to join a good track coming in on your left. Turn right and go on up.

From now on an obvious path, involving occasional small scrambles, takes you up the switchback slopes, known as The Edge. Each prominent hillock ahead seems like the summit, but once it is surmounted, another lies beyond. But after an exciting climb the pyramidal top of Ullock Pike is attained.

The views are breathtaking, with all of Bassenthwaite Lake

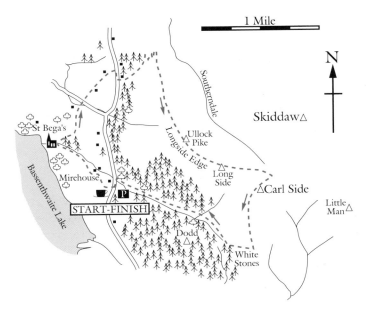

and much of Derwent Water revealed below. The Galloway hills, across the low land of north-west Cumbria and the Solway, appear just a short distance away. To your left are the forbidding and almost vertical slopes of Skiddaw, with the lonely, remote Southerndale at its foot.

Continue on along the wide, airy ridge, known as Longside Edge, to its cairn. Beyond stroll on the cairned way to a junction of paths. Turn right to ascend, gently, the wide track up onto the domed, undistinguished summit of Carl Side. Beyond, go on the descending track until you reach a largish area of outcropping quartz boulders, named White Stones on the OS map.

Pause here to rest your knees after the long downhill way and to enjoy the magnificent view. Then turn right to follow the path for two cairns. Then descend left through heather and cowberry to a stile into Dodd forest. Turn right and stride the forest road. Ignore the acute left turn to the top of the Dodd and also the next left turn. A few yards on take the next left branch to follow the green banded posts. These lead you downhill through the mixed woodland to The Sawmill teashop.

THE COFFEE LOUNGE

Visit an ancient stone circle after strolling the delightful Keswick Railway footpath as it dallies delectably with the River Greta.

DISTANCE: 6 miles (10km)
TIME: 3-4 hours
MAP: OS OL 4
TERRAIN: Easy walking all the way.
PARKING: Long stay pay-and-display car park in centre of Keswick. GR 266236.

The Coffee Lounge in Lupton Court stands beside the short-stay car park (maximum stay 3 hours). It opens seven days a week from 9.30am to 5pm all year through, excepting Christmas Day. It is a large, cheery teashop with a fine view of Latrigg. There are tables outside edging Lupton Court. All the food is homemade.

During the Industrial Revolution, and most of the 19th century, the iron-ore mines of West Cumberland were expanding rapidly. Although coal was mined locally it was not suitable for smelting, so most of the ore was sent by train on a circuitous route via Carlisle to the blast furnaces of the north-east. The trains returned with coke from Durham coalfields for the growing number of furnaces. A new railway was needed to provide a more direct route between the east and west coast. The new line, the Cockermouth, Keswick and Penrith railway, was completed in 1864. Sadly, it was closed in 1972, a casualty of the lorry and the car. The pleasing footpath was created in the 1980s by the Lake District National Park Authority.

THE COFFEE LOUNGE

K E S W I C K

From the long-stay car park, turn left (the Coffee Lounge now lies to your right) and walk to the traffic lights at the road corner to follow the signpost for the Leisure Centre. Turn left down Station Road and, just before it curves right, look left for the Railway Footpath signpost, directing you to the right of the Leisure Centre. Beyond, bear right to come to the platform of Keswick's old station.

Stroll the level way to cross the River Greta by a sturdy bridge, an inverted 'bowstring' constructed of steel girders. Continue on the hedged way to where the track unexpectedly climbs steeply for a short distance. This is where trains emerged from the 'Big Tunnel'.

Go on to pass under the viaduct which carries the A66. Descend the steps that take you to the side of the Greta and the siding of Low Briery. Dawdle on to cross more bridges over the river, some inverted bowstrings and others upright. A mile-and-a-half from the station, on the right, is a small stone hut with information boards.

Continue on to cross the next bridge, near the confluence of the Glenderaterra Beck with the Greta. Beyond, a signposted stile on the right leads to a permitted footpath to Castlerigg stone circle. The path climbs a pasture to the A66, which you cross (with care). Then walk right a few yards to a signposted path that climbs to the side of the old road.

Bear left and walk on to take the first right and then the next right. Go on along the road to pass Goose Well Farm and then on to come to the entrance to the Castlerigg Stone Circle on your left.

The circle may have been used as a meeting place for bartering livestock, exchanging partners or celebrating tribal festivals. It may also have been used to calculate the cycle of seasons – vital for local farmers. It was probably built between BC 2300 and 1300.

Leave the site, turn right and walk back for 50 yards to take the footpath, signposted The Nest, on the right. Stride the wide, clear way over pastures, to climb three ladderstiles. Pass through a gate to walk to the right of High Nest. Carry on along its access track to come to the side of the A591. Cross and turn right to walk 50 yards, uphill, to a gate on the left, signposted Walla Crag.

Walk ahead, with a fence to your right and a fine view of Helvellyn over the valley to your left. Climb the next two stiles, still with the boundary to your right. Head on to a ladderstile on the right – the signpost is on the opposite side. Beyond, go on with the wall to your right through the delightful high pastures.

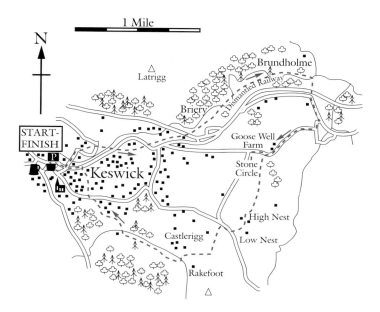

Continue to a narrow road, where you turn left and, after ten yards, take the signposted kissing gate on your right. Drop down steps and walk on to cross a footbridge over Brockle Beck. Follow the delightful path as it bears right through a deciduous copse, with the beck soon to be lost to sight on your right as the gill through which it tumbles becomes deeper and deeper. The path climbs gently to a brow and ahead is a wonderful view of Derwent Water, often called the 'Queen of the Lakes'.

Follow the path as it descends steadily towards the lake, ignoring the track that goes off right. Keep to the right of Springs Farm and go on along Springs Road to come to Ambleside Road. Turn left and walk on to Eskin

Street, where you turn right. At the main Penrith road, turn left and walk on to cross Southey Road to come to the traffic lights at the start of the walk. Head on to the short stay car park and the Coffee Lounge.

LAKESIDE TEA GARDENS

E njoy strolling the low-level paths beside the lake and climbing the way onto Walla Crag and Castle Head.

DISTANCE: 6 miles (10km) or 3½ miles (6km)
TIME: 3 hours or 2 hours
MAP: OS OL 4
TERRAIN: Easy underfoot. Steady climb onto Castle Head and through Great Wood onto Walla Crag.
PARKING: Pay-and-display car park close to the landing stages on Derwent Water. GR 265229.

The Lakeside Tea Gardens are aptly named, with many tables set out along flower-lined terraces. The café sits in a hollow sheltered on three sides by forest trees and set on a small eminence, above the terraces, with a beautiful view that all can enjoy. Walkers and their gear are warmly welcomed; their dogs must be kept on leads in the gardens. The café opens seven days a week from the beginning of March until the end of November. It then opens at weekends only and during the Christmas holidays. It serves delicious food from 9am to 6pm in the summer and 10am to 5pm in the winter.

The islands on the lake are seen from much of this walk. In the 18th century, the eccentric Joseph Pocklington lived on Derwent Isle, the nearest island seen from Friar's Crag. He organised regattas, which included a mock sea battle. Further along the lake is Lord's Isle. Here lived Lord Derwentwater, a Jacobite, who was beheaded on Tower Hill, London. Legend has it that his young wife fled, with the family's jewels, up Lady's

*Rake, a steep gully (not attempted on this walk) that leads
on to Walla Crag. Beyond Lord's Isle lies Rampsholme
Island and west of it is St Herbert's Island, the home of the
7th century saint. Friar's Crag is believed to be named
after the friars who waited for a boat to take them across to
see the hermit. St Herbert's is the island that Squirrel
Nutkin visited in Beatrix Potter's book of the same name.
In the 17th century German miners employed to extract
'wad' (see walk 10) from nearby mines were not welcomed
by the locals and preferred to live in isolation on the islands.*

From the car park, turn left to pass The Lakeside Tea
Gardens on your left, the landing stages on the right and
then Cockshot Wood on the left. At the road end take the
signposted footpath to continue on to Friar's Crag. Pass

the plaque dedicated to Canon Rawnsley, a founder of the National Trust. Dawdle on along the path through the trees to see the fine memorial to John Ruskin, who was devoted to preserving the beauty of the Lake District. Continue to the end of the crag to enjoy one of Lakeland's glorious views.

Return a few yards along the path and bear right down steps to a gate on the right. Press on along the lakeshore and follow the waymarked path as it swings inland to enter Ings Wood. Go over a footbridge and then emerge from the trees by a gate, where you turn right. Waymarks direct you back to the shore of Calf Close Bay. The delightful path then enters more woodland and passes through a yew copse.

Leave the trees and carry on along the shore. Look for a huge boulder that has been split in two – each exposed surface has an intricate pattern carved on it. Just beyond the boulder, walk away from the lake to pass through a gap stile to cross, with care, the Borrowdale Road. Go through the gap stile opposite and walk right, parallel with the road.

Head up a small slope to a parking area with picnic tables, set among the trees of Great Wood. Pass through the gate at the back of the car park, signposted Ashness Bridge and Walla Crag.

Bear right and almost immediately left to take the signposted track for Walla Crag via Rakefoot. The way climbs steadily uphill through larch, eventually levelling out, keeping below the seemingly unassailable face of Walla Crag.

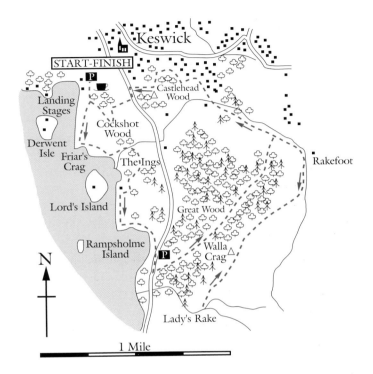

At a division of the track, keep to the signposted right fork and carry on to leave the woodland by a stile. Go on ahead and, at the side of the deep gill through which flows Brockle Beck, you have a choice. You can either turn left to return to the lake (see route later in text) or walk right to go up on Walla Crag.

Stroll upstream of the pretty beck to a footbridge. Beyond it, you climb steps to a kissing gate to a narrow road. Turn right and, at the Y-junction, take the right branch. At the end of the tarmac recross the beck by another footbridge.

Bear left up a confusion of tracks, keeping parallel with the wall on your right. Go with the wall as it turns right. Stride up the pasture, with the trees on top of the Crag now inviting you onwards. Ignore the first gate in the wall and, a few yards on, take the next one, which gives access, safely, to the exposed edge of the immense crag. Pause here to enjoy the magnificent view.

Press on to take, on the left, a grassy path through heather. This soon comes beside the fell wall. Follow this until you reach a gated stile onto Low Moss, where you turn left. Stride beside the wall until you rejoin your outward route.

Then retrace your steps, down the slope, over the two footbridges and along the narrow path beside the stream, which is now on your right. Soon you reach the junction with the path from Great Wood, coming in on your left, and where you made your route decision.

Go on down and down to pass to the right of Springs Farm to join a metalled road. Walk on for a quarter-of-a-mile. Look for the signposted hedged track (easy to miss) that goes off left, opposite a house named Wood Close. Take the kissing gate into Castlehead Wood and climb some steps.

Walk ahead, ignoring the left and right turns. Where the track turns right, go on uphill through the splendid woodland. You will have to scramble a little to reach the summit viewpoint, from where you can see the entire length of Derwent Water.

Return to the main path and walk left to come to a stile to the road. Cross Borrowdale Road, bear left and take the signposted footpath directing you towards the lake. Enter Cockshot Wood, bear left and follow the track round to join the road at the landing stages. Walk right for the tea gardens and the car park.

GRANGE B'DGE COTTAGE

B O R R O W D A L E

O n this walk you climb high to visit a monument and enjoy a spectacular view, and bend low to enter the cave home of a self-styled Professor of Adventure.

DISTANCE:
4¹/₂ miles
(7.5km)
TIME: 3 hours
MAP: OS OL 4
TERRAIN: The
path to the
monument is
reached by a
rather rugged
ascent. Easy
walking for the
rest of the way.
PARKING: A
very small
parking area, on
the right, just
over Grange
Bridge. GR
253175.

Picturesque Grange Bridge Cottage is 400 years old. It serves teas indoors, and in two areas out-of-doors, at tables in front of the cottage and in a small garden behind it, beside the River Derwent. It opens from 10am to 7.30pm, seven days a week for most of the year, closing for three weeks after January 7 and also on Christmas Day and Boxing Day. All the food is made on the premises. Tel. 017687 77201.

In the 13th century the village of Grange was a grange, or granary, for the monks of Furness Abbey, who bought Derwent Water in 1209. Visit the small church with its fine barrel roof. It was built, early in the 19th century, by Margaret Heathcote, an indomitable lady who expected women and girls to curtsey when she passed and men and boys to touch their forelocks. She is reputed to have kept her white coffin in her house for several years ready for her death.

Walk in front of the tearooms and go on to take a narrow road, on your

left, signposted Rosthwaite. Where the lane swings right
to Hollows Farm go on ahead along the continuing
track, which is walled to the left. Continue to come to
the side of the wide, surging River Derwent.

Cross two footbridges over feeder streams and bear right
to follow the signposted directions for Seatoller and
Honister, to climb a rough track that ascends steadily.
Well before the brow of the hill you come to a huge
mound of quarry waste below pine-crowned Castle Crag.
Just beyond, watch out for the large cairn, on the left,
that marks your route to the memorial. The route starts
off as a grassy trod and soon becomes reinforced. A seat
at its first bend commemorates Agnes, the wife of Sir
William Hamer, who gave the surrounding land to the
nation.

Continue up the well-pitched path to a stile. Beyond bear

right to just before a ladderstile (your return route). Do not cross but bear left to go on ascending, with care, an enormous mound of quarry waste. Soon you reach a grassy, flat area by some quarrymen's huts, now derelict. Pause to enjoy the grand view.

Go on up a narrow, well-trodden path, under scattered trees and then over grass. Wind round the edge of a quarried hollow, to your left, to come to a plaque fixed to a huge boulder. It says that Castle Crag was given to the National Trust in 1920 by Sir William Hamer in memory of John Hamer, killed in action in the 1914-18 war, and of ten Borrowdale men who also died.

The view is astounding. Borrowdale lies at your feet. The crag was the site of a small hill fort, possibly Celtic, although Roman pottery has been found here. As you stand and marvel at the vista you realise that the fort was built at a wonderfully strategic point in the valley and must have been nigh on impregnable – even though the attackers would not have had to toil up the spoil heap!

Descend to the second ladderstile on your left, ignored on your upward route. Cross and follow the narrow path, with a fence to your left, through outcrops to return to the track, on your right, once more. Stride on over the brow and, just beyond the corner of the last fence, drop left, over a slope, to a gate. Follow the clear, grassy way downhill to a stile. Then head for the bottom right corner to a gate. Once through, turn left to take, immediately, the gate on your left.

Follow the path over a pasture and into the deciduous woodland that clothes the slopes below Castle Crag.

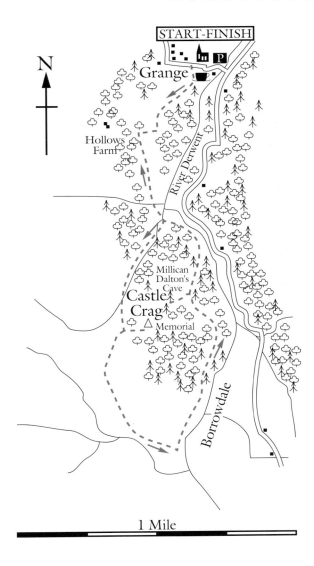

1 Mile

Continue on as the path moves away from the river and begins to pass through quarry waste, softened with moss and birch. At the point where the path climbs steadily and before it swings sharp right, take the narrow but clear track off left.

It passes through an old quarry and then winds left and right to pass, on the left, a quarry cave, which you ignore. Go on to a very large cave on your left.

This is where Millican Dalton, the 'Professor of Adventure', lived for much of his life. He made his own clothes and used an old bicycle as a barrow for transporting his needs. Go inside the cave, which he used as his living quarters. To the right is a smaller cave, a second storey, where he slept.

Return to the main path and turn left to continue on the well-marked path. Go through a wall gap and follow a slated causeway right. Stroll on to join the track taken on your outward route. It leads you back to Grange and its cottage teashop.

FLOCK IN TEAROOM

This gentle walk takes you into the depths of a rugged valley deep in Borrowdale, a magnificent reward for a modest output of energy.

DISTANCE:
4¹/₂ miles (7km)
TIME: 3-4
hours
MAP: OS OL 4
TERRAIN:
Generally easy,
level walking.
PARKING:
National Trust
pay-and-display
car park in lane
off the B5289 as
it passes
through
Rosthwaite
village. GR
258148.

The small Flock In at Rosthwaite was once the stable of Yew Tree farm. It was set up by the owner especially for walkers, the tiled floor coping well with muddy boots and wet rucksacks. There is a pretty flower garden with tables, where dogs are welcome, and bench seats in front of the tearoom, on the lane. Fine china half-pint and pint mugs provide an excellent cuppa. All the food is homemade and the giant flapjacks and 'flock-in-slices' are memorable. Open seven days a week from Easter, 10am-5pm, to the middle of November. Open for the spring half-term. Tel. 01768 777675.

Before 1750 horse-drawn sledges provided the only transport in and around Rosthwaite. This was the way that Francis Herries, founder of the dynasty described in Hugh Walpole's novels, brought his family into Borrowdale in 1730. Two decades later wheeled carts were used, but a century passed before a road was constructed. During the 18th and 19th centuries, when travel difficulties made the village remote from Keswick, the townsfolk referred to the villagers

47

as 'gowks', or cuckoos. Legend had it that the villagers built a wall across the valley to keep the cuckoo in, believing that in this way they would prevent the return of winter and harsh weather.

Turn left out of the car park and stroll ahead to the B-road that runs through the valley. Cross, and walk left to take, on your right, the signposted footpath, part of the Cumbria Way, following the directions for Stonethwaite. Go over the footbridge and turn right.

The delightful walled track continues beside the Stonethwaite Beck as it hurries below birch and sycamore. It comes close to a small island with a pleasing stone seat on which to dally. Then go on along the gated, walled way and continue where the path moves out into open pastures. Over the wall lies the hamlet of Stonethwaite.

Stay on the track as you move deeper into the lovely valley. Pass a small plantation of larch, all with elegant, drooping branches. Ahead tower the dramatic slopes of Bleak How, Heron Crag and Sergeant's Crag. Cross a footbridge and stroll on. Galleny Force lies to your right, over a fence and almost out of sight. Save your viewing of this lovely fall for your return.

Pass four water wracks, placed across a boulder-strewn gill, which allow the stream to join the Stonethwaite Beck without taking debris with it. A few yards on look right for the footbridge over the Stonethwaite and as you

cross read its moving commemoration. Beyond walk right, with care, to view a tiny gorge, where the Langstrath Beck unites with the Stonethwaite. The way, now a narrow path, proceeds along the east side, and generally parallel with, the Langstrath. Continue on to a footbridge over the beck. Cross and turn right to begin your return below birch, ash and holly. Go through a gate to pass under ancient oaks and, just before the start of a walled track, bear right to walk across a pasture towards the noise of Galleny force.

Pause here to enjoy the lovely waterfall as it descends in a turquoise cascade topped with white foam. Climb the stile and continue beside the beck. Go on to climb a high ladderstile up the slope. The good path continues ahead, with a spectacular view of the High Spy range of fells. Follow the clear, stiled path over the pastures to come to the side of the Langstrath Country Inn.

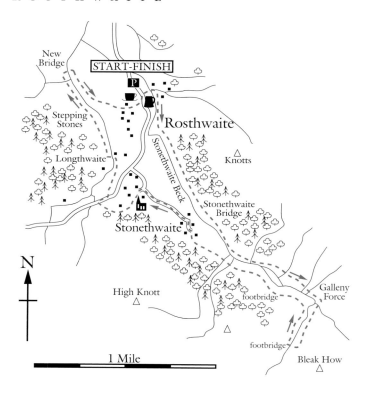

Walk ahead through the pretty hamlet, and on along the narrow road, to turn left at the signpost, directing you to Borrowdale Road, via Chapel Farm. Pass the church and wind round left of the cottages beyond, to walk a walled track. This leads to a three-armed signpost, where you turn right to take a stile onto the B-road. Turn right and, in 50 yards, climb the stile, which has a signpost pointing the way to Rosthwaite.

Cross a pasture to a ladderstile and, beyond, continue edging right of a curious, long, grassy mound to a step stile, which gives access to a narrow path. Turn right to join the road and walk left, following it as it winds left to cross a fine bridge over the River Derwent. Turn right to walk through a farmyard and then the continuing fenced path beside the river. Stroll on along this glorious path to cross it by stepping stones, or by the charming New Bridge, further along. Both of these lead you by walled tracks to the Flock In, where a choice of Earl Grey or Yorkshire Tea awaits you. The parking area lies a short distance beyond.

THE YEW TREE

I n late spring, with a multitude of wild flowers colouring the pastures and verges, and spring migrants proclaiming their territories, this walk is heaven indeed.

DISTANCE: 5¹/₂ miles (9km) Could be shortened to 3 miles (5km)
TIME: 3 hours or 1¹/₂ hours
MAP: OS OL 4
TERRAIN: Easy walking most of the way, with a steepish climb out of Seatoller.
PARKING: Pay-and-display car park at Seatoller. GR 245138.

The Yew Tree was originally two cottages built in 1628 and occupied by German miners in the time of Queen Elizabeth I to extract 'wad' (see below) from the mines. Many of the original features of the building, such as mellowed oak beams, slate floor, open range and brick bread oven, have been retained. The restaurant nestles at the foot of the Borrowdale end of the Honister Pass. It opens seven days a week from Easter to the October half-term. In winter it closes in January and on Mondays. Opening times are from 10am to 5pm. Walkers are greatly welcomed but must take their dogs into the charming garden with its several picnic tables. The food is made on the premises and the "rum nicky" has most restorative properties. Tel. 017687 77634.

'Wad' was the local name for black lead, or plumbago or graphite, and had, since the 16th century, been obtained from the fellside above Seathwaite. It was used in medicines, dyes and mouldings for cannon balls, shot and bombs. It was also used for pencils, which were produced locally. It

*is believed that even earlier shepherds used wad to mark
their sheep. It was so valuable that miners leaving work
were searched, and once an armed attack was made on the
mining offices. By the 19th century the deposits were
exhausted.*

From the car park, turn right to walk the narrow road
through the hamlet of Seatoller, passing The Yew Tree on
your left. Where the road turns sharply left, climb to a
gate on the right. Walk ahead beside the wall on your
right and then follow the path as it swings away left.
Cross a wide cycle track (the old toll road) and continue
up the arrowed way to a waymarked gate in the wall.

Turn right along the foot of High Scawdel. Cross the footbridge over Scaleclose Gill and the next one over several small streams that drain the slopes above. Continue through a gate and then go on the pleasing way to just before the next beck, Tongue Gill, which hurries down the fellside.

Leave the main path and pass through a gate on the right to descend a grassy way, with Tongue Beck noisily descending under luxuriant vegetation to your left. At the ladderstile on your right, do not cross but bear left to walk a grassy path that returns you to the side of the gill. Where there is a choice of paths, choose the one beside the beck. Go on downhill to the stile in the bottom right corner.

Beyond, stroll on with the beck to your left, to cross a small footbridge. Ignore the ford on your left, climb a ladderstile and then the next stile at the confluence of the beck with the River Derwent. Turn right to cross a footbridge and walk on.

The narrow path continues, delectably, beside a fine stretch of the tree-lined river, to pass in front of Longthwaite farmhouse. Cross over its access road and go on ahead to pass the youth hostel on your right. Stride on below oaks beside the river, now boulder-strewn and turbulent.

Take care as you clamber over the boulders above the river and, towards the end of the way, use the chain to help you balance. Do not bear off right but keep ahead, and beyond the last boulder a hidden path is suddenly

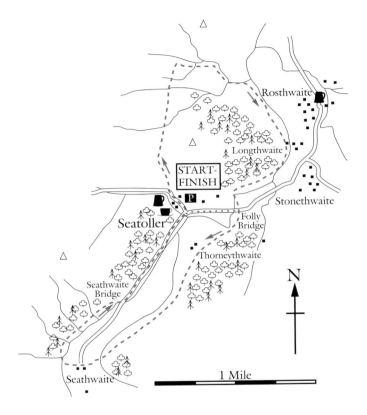

revealed. Turn right.

Dawdle the lovely way through Johnny Wood to a gate onto a pasture. The wide path goes on to pass through a gap in the wall on the left. Here, if you wish to return to Seatoller follow the path, right, walking on in the same general direction, the way bringing you to the car park and then The Yew Tree.

To continue the walk bear left to cross the footbridge over the river and stroll ahead to the valley road. Cross and go on along a gated track, signposted Seathwaite. Ignore both footpaths off left and stroll on along a reinforced, walled track. Watch out for the continuation of the way, a narrow path, walled on one side and fenced on the other. Climb the pleasing stile and go on through the valley.

Notice the huge boulders incorporated into the footings of the wall as you continue on the gated way below Thornythwaite Fell on your left. From here you have a good view of Sourmilk Gill waterfall, one of three in the Lake District with the same name. Follow the clear path and track to the tiny hamlet of Seathwaite, which has the unenviable title of the wettest place in Lakeland. Turn right and, in a few yards, pass left through an arch (it is signposted but this is difficult to spot). Walk ahead towards the glorious waterfall.

Cross the sturdy footbridge over the Derwent. Bear right to go over a second bridge. Walk ahead and take note of the engraved stone set in the footpath and puzzle over the wilful destroyer of an earlier one. Pass through a gate and go on along the stony path close to the delightful river.

The way ends all too soon at the side of the valley road. Turn left and walk the narrow way to return to Seatoller.

HEUGHSCAR TEA ROOMS

High above the village of Pooley Bridge is just the place for a brisk, stimulating walk, following the old Roman Road, High Street – which, when it was first trodden by soldiers' feet, was no doubt endured rather than enjoyed.

DISTANCE: 7 miles (12km)
TIME: 3-4 hours
MAP: OS OL 5
TERRAIN: Very good walking on clear tracks and paths.
PARKING: Either car park in village. GR 470246.

Heughscar Tea Rooms has a lawn sloping down to the river, with white tables and chairs set about it. It has flower gardens full of colour. It is named after the limestone hill seen to your left on the walk, just after you pass Roehead Farm. A manuscript displayed on a wall says that the teashop was bought for £150 in 1860. It once had its own jetty on the river. Walkers, including their boots and rucksacks, are made most welcome. Dogs can be taken into the garden. The tearoom is open from March to November between 10am and 5pm. Tel 017684 86453.

Pooley Bridge lies at the foot of Ullswater and is within the national park. The 16th century bridge, after which the village is named, spans the river where it emerges from the lake. Pooley means 'a mound by a pool' and once there was a large pool in the river, long since removed by dredging. Above the village stands the thickly-wooded hill Dunmallard.

Walk into the village square, passing

the teashop on your left. Continue past St Paul's Church, which was built in 1868, and the village hall, dating from 1912. Take the right turn for Howtown and Martindale and go on over crossroads. Stride ahead in the direction of Roehead, along a tree-lined lane. Look right for your first magnificent view of Ullswater and the fine mountains that crowd the head of the lake.

Pass Roehead Farm on the left and go through the gate ahead, which gives access to Barton Fell Common. Stride the wide track as it climbs gently up onto the moorland, where in summer curlew, skylark, meadow pipit and green plover nest.

Ignore all turnings until you reach a four-armed signpost. Here bear right to follow the route of the Roman Road, and in the direction of Howtown. Near a junction of

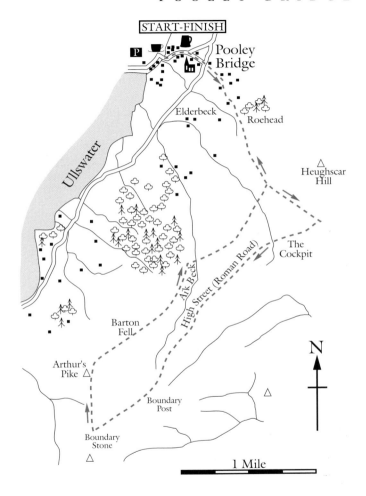

paths, look left to see a stone circle and then take a path going off right. A hundred yards along, close to a cairn, cross a shallow ditch to reach a junction of paths. The right branch leads towards the lake. Take the left branch, the Roman Road.

This springy, grassy way climbs steadily south west up onto lonely Barton Fell. Enjoy the splendid views of Blencathra to your right and the Howgills to your left. Pause and look back to see a long, forbidding stretch of the Pennines. After a mile-and-a-quarter you reach, on your left, a boundary stone. Once it would have stood proud but today it is propped up by a pile of stones. Near here you might spot evidence of badgers.

Stride on along the clear way, where you feel you must hear marching feet, to, on your right, the next boundary stone. Here the main stone lies horizontal, surrounded by boulders. A hundred yards further on, at a junction of paths, turn acute right to walk a good path through heather, which avoids the pools and bogs of this wild upland area. The path soon becomes a track and leads to the left of a cairned hillock. At a large cairn, take the narrow path on the left which leads you to the top of Arthur's Pike (1,800 feet/550m). A dramatic view awaits.

Take a similar narrow path across the moorland to rejoin the main path by a second large cairn. Turn left to descend the wide, exhilarating, grassy trod all the way to the fell wall. Turn right along a track that leads you into Aik Gill and to convenient stones on which to step across the hurrying stream. Climb up the opposite bank and follow the continuing path across the moorland to join the track taken on your outward route.

Turn left to retrace your steps to the village and Heughscar Tea Rooms.

AIRA FORCE TEA ROOMS

V isit Aira Force before starting off to rub shoulders with Helvellyn, returning over the lovely slopes of Glencoyne Park.

DISTANCE:
6½ miles
(10km)
TIME: 3-4
hours
MAP: OS OL 5
TERRAIN:
Stones can be slippery around Aira Force.
Open fell walk.
PARKING: The Aira Force pay-and-display car park on the A592 just east of the A5091.
GR 401201.

The Aira Force tea rooms, set idyllically under trees, is open from mid-March to early November and during Christmas, from 10am to 5.30pm. It has tables outside which overlook Ullswater. Walkers, straight from the fells, are made very welcome but dogs must be left outside. Tel. 017684 82262.

The peaceful valley of Matterdale runs from the Penrith-Keswick road to the shores of Ullswater. Its name comes from 'madderdock', a red-rooted plant which was once used as a dye. The 16th century hotel at Dockray was a coaching inn and it is said that Mary, Queen of Scots, stayed here, and also William and Dorothy Wordsworth.

Leave by the gate at the back of the car park, which is signposted 'Pinetum and waterfalls'. Follow the path as it swings right to cross two footbridges, with The Glade and its inviting seats to your left. Where the track forks, take the lower branch, which leads into the narrowing

ravine. At the next footbridge you have a spectacular view of Aira Force – one of Lakeland's most dramatic and popular waterfalls.

Walk back a few yards and climb the steep steps, now on your left, to cross the narrow, arched bridge over the magnificent falls. Go right to continue. Cross the next footbridge over a narrow gorge, bear left and walk above the beck. Through the holly and birch you will see a white wall of water, the Upper Force. Continue along the clear, gated path through woodland, following the signs to Dockray and Ulcat Row to emerge onto bracken-covered fell. At the three-armed signpost, take the track for Dockray, passing the dwellings of Millses and Hollins to join the A5091.

Cross the A-road and walk the narrow fell road, which passes in front of the Royal Hotel. Carry on towards High Row and Dowthwaitehead. After half-a-mile look left for the footpath sign, just beyond the gate through which you pass. The one-and-a-half miles to Dowthwaite is well stiled and gated, with waymarks, and no instructions are needed.

The white-painted farmhouse at Dowthwaite lies close up against Dowthwaite Crag. At this point, turn left to cross the sturdy footbridge over the Aira Beck. Pass through the gate on the right and continue ahead beside the wall on your left. Where it swings away left, look for the waymark directing you on and between two large, grassy hummocks. Press on, now continuing along a raised way to a gate onto the open fell.

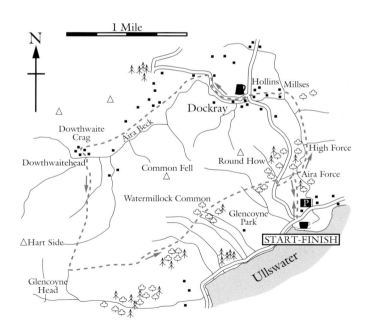

Continue straight up for 150 yards from the gate, beside a small stream, and then bear left. Continue steadily, and slightly right, skirting Birkett Fell to your right, with Watermillock Common stretching away, featurelessly, to your left.

Cross two narrow streams and go on in the same general direction to pass through a ruined wall. From here you can enjoy dramatic views of Glencoyne Head, Catstye Cam and Helvellyn. Carry on and then begin to descend, quite steeply, to join a path coming in on your right from Glencoyne Head.

Turn left to walk the narrow shelf-like way above slopes which drop even more steeply to Glencoyne Beck. Pass back through the fell wall once again, though this time 250 yards further south. Stride on and enjoy Ullswater, now coming into view. As you near another wall on your right, continue beside it to a large, man-made gap. Go through and follow the clear, rapidly descending green path, past wizened larch. Continue as it zigzags and then levels out above a beech wood.

At the end of the trees a stile gives access to a distinct and pleasing footpath, which traverses the fell for about a mile above Glencoyne park. This returns you to a stile onto the A5091, opposite a small car park, through which you walk. Descend the steeply stepped and gated way through larch for another fine view of Aira Force. Follow the path as it swings right and ever downwards until you stand on the footbridge below the fall. Return to the car park by your outward route and take a path on the right which leads to the teashop and a cuppa.

KAREN'S KITCHEN

G *lenridding on Ullswater is a delightful village from which to start a walk.*

DISTANCE:
First footbridge
5 miles (8km),
second 6 miles
(10km),
Grisedale Tarn 8
miles (13km);
to include the
circuit of the
tarn, 9 miles
(14.5km)
TIME: 3, 3$^1/_2$,
4, 4$^1/_2$ hours
MAP: OS OL 5
TERRAIN: The
path to the tarn
is stony and
uneven
underfoot.
PARKING: Pay-
and-display car
park in the
village. GR
386169.

Karen's Lakeland Kitchen has tables outside and beyond a low wall hurries Glenridding Beck. It is a vegetarian teashop and all the delicious food is prepared on the premises. Walkers, their boots and rucksacks, are most welcome, and well behaved dogs are allowed into the first of two rooms. From Easter to November it is open seven days a week from 10.30am to 5pm. It is closed on Christmas Day and Boxing Day and open weekends in the winter, depending on the weather. On one wall is an enormous map of the Lake District, in relief. Tel. 017684 82392.

Glenridding lies on the shores of Ullswater and is geared to tourism. Three hundred years ago it was a mining village and it had one of the most successful lead mines in England, producing many thousands of tons of lead, plus a little silver. The mine is claimed to be 3,000 feet at its deepest part. In 1959 it was used to test instruments for detecting underground atomic explosions. During a great storm in October 1927 the dam above the mine burst,

65

*sending a great flood of water down the valley, causing
enormous damage. Miraculously, no human life was lost. It
is said that the water swept into the basement of a hotel,
where the maids were sleeping. Their beds floated to the
ceiling. Fortunately a window burst open and allowed them
to escape.*

From the car park return to the A592, turn right and
cross Glenridding Bridge. Turn right again to walk past
Karen's Lakeland Kitchen, one of a row of shops, on
your left. Pass the public hall and Eagle Farm. At the
signpost turn left for Lanty's Tarn to pass through
deciduous woodland. At the next signpost take the left
fork and begin a steady climb through alders.

Continue climbing and pause on a seat, with a good view
of the lake. Go on through a kissing gate and walk
ahead. Ignore the gate ahead and turn sharp left to climb
more gently along a pitched path.

Then the path levels out and pretty Lanty's Tarn lies
ahead, edged with Scots pine. Once it provided ice for
Patterdale Hall.

Continue on past the end of the pool to stroll the
descending track to a gate in a wall corner. Beyond go
through a gate on the left to descend over pasture to an
access road. Go on ahead to cross Grisedale Beck and
join a narrow road, where you turn right. Saunter the
gated way in the direction of Grasmere and Grisedale
Tarn. Pass Elmhow Farm and then Elmhow Barn,

following the sign that directs walkers to the gate on the left of the building. Ahead is a glorious view of the mountains about the dale and the white-topped Nethermostcove Beck racing downwards from a remote hollow.

The clear track continues beside Crossing Plantation and then out over open fell. Now you can see Ruthwaite Beck descending below High Crag. Here you might wish to return by dropping down the slope on the right to a footbridge over the Grisedale and turning right to return to Glenridding.

To extend the walk, stride on through the valley, climbing a gentle slope into a lonely hollow. Follow the way as it descends steadily to cross a footbridge over the hurrying Grisedale, passing under a solitary ash tree. The rough path continues over a wettish area. Here you can bear

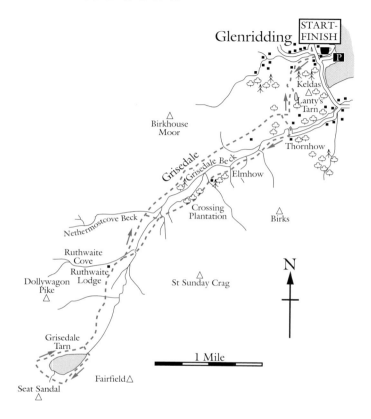

right to cross a tractor bridge over Ruthwaite Beck to return to Glenridding.

To reach Grisedale Tarn, do not cross the tractor bridge but continue uphill on the now rocky track towards Ruthwaite Lodge, a small climbing hut. Go on along the clear but rough path. Gradually it begins to climb and crosses two boulder fields to come close to a large cairn. At the next cairn the way becomes easier but still rough. Suddenly the picturesque tarn lies before you. Here you might wish to walk clockwise around the silvery pool.

Ahead lies the grassy top of Seat Sandal. As you near the skirt of this bulky fell, look left (south) to see a rough slope descending from the summit of Fairfield. Then as you wind round the tarn you can see the eroded, zigzagging path up Dollywagon Pike. Continue on to rejoin your outward path and return along the rough way to the climbing lodge.

From here the narrow, grassy path continues more easily, with a delightful view of the dale ahead. Pass through a gate close to the foot of an enormously long wall that stretches steeply up towards Striding Edge.

Continue on high above the vale, with the beck to your right, to pass through three more gates to descend to the wall corner encountered on your outward route. Ignore the gate on your right, taken earlier, and go through the kissing gate to ascend towards Lanty's Tarn. Retrace your outward route to Glenridding and Karen's Lakeland Kitchen.

THE ROWAN TREE

A lcock Tarn nestles in a hidden hollow in the hills and is attained by an exhilarating climb.

DISTANCE: 4 miles (6.5km)
TIME: 2-3 hours
MAP: OS OL 7
TERRAIN: Pleasant paths across the valley floor. Steep and rough but delightful climb to the tarn. The descent is steep.
PARKING: Grasmere has several car parks; this walk starts from the one behind the Information Centre. GR 336074.

The popular Rowan Tree, which warmly welcomes walkers – their boots, rucksacks and waterproofs – has had to move to bigger premises. Today it stands in an idyllic spot, its terrace of outdoor tables edging the River Rothay in the heart of vibrant Grasmere. Here your dog can join you. As you drink your tea and eat your homemade cookies, watch for trout and a variety of birds that haunt the river. A small rowan grows valiantly in the paved riverside area. The teashop is open all year except for Christmas Day, Boxing Day and the last three weeks in January. Visit during 10am-5pm and 6pm-9pm. Tel. 015394 35528.

St Oswald's church, Grasmere, is dedicated to the Northumbrian king who was killed at the battle of Masserfield in AD 642. In its churchyard are yews planted by the poet William Wordsworth and here too is his grave and those of his wife and daughter. The poet's beloved sister, Dorothy, is buried close by. Wordsworth and his sister moved into a house at Town End in December 1799. Today it is known as Dove

Cottage and is passed on the outward leg of this walk.

Head towards the church and turn right in front of it to pass The Rowan Tree. Turn left onto a signposted footpath to go in front of the primary school. Continue on. Ignore the kissing gate on the left (your return route) and follow the track, right, to cross the valley floor. Take care as you continue over the A591. Turn right and stride for 440 yards to take the left turn to pass Dove Cottage.

Climb the gently sloping hill and, just before a pond, bear left along a narrow footpath that winds over common land to a seat. Walk left in the direction of Alcock Tarn along the reinforced way. By a National

Trust sign for Brackenfell you are confronted by two paths. Take the one on the right and climb steeply between two walls to a kissing gate.

Beyond, the stony way continues ever upwards, keeping parallel with the wall to your left. Take lots of pauses to look back on a grand view of Loughrigg and its cave and

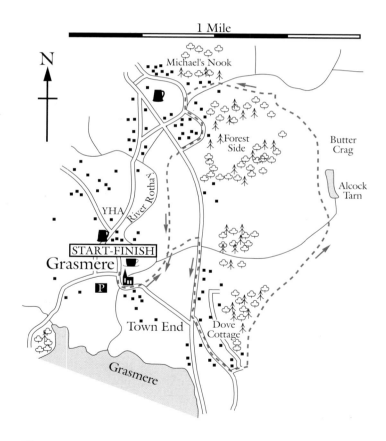

of Silver How. After just over half-a-mile, and a few yards before the wall finally turns away left, take the step stile on your left, beside which is a fine dog gate.

Step across a small stream that has issued out of the tarn and stroll along a wide, grassy way. Keep right of Grey Crags, where you might spot the socket for the flag used for the guides' race in the Grasmere Sports. Over the small, dammed end of the tarn, descends a waterfall.

The tarn is named after Ralph Henry Alcock, who was the proprietor of the Hollins House Hotel in about the late 1840s. He enlarged the mountain pool and stocked it with trout. It was once called Butter Crag Tarn after the crag of the same name at the head of the pool. It is a pleasing and welcoming sight after the long toil upwards and just the place for a laze in the sun.

Carry on, with the tarn to your right, to a stile. Beyond, head on along the clear path, first beside a wet area before it begins to descend steeply towards Greenhead Gill. The path zigzags down to a walled plantation. Follow the wall right with increasingly delightful views down into the gill.

Remain by the forest wall all the way to cross a footbridge over the beck. Turn left to walk the continuing delectable, tarmacked way, now on the right of the stream. At the T-junction turn left and take the next left. Follow this right to join the A591, with Our Lady of the Wayside church (1964) to your left. It is well worth a visit. Cross the road and walk left for 50 yards to take the well signposted footpath, right, over the meadows to Grasmere and The Rowan Tree.

RATTLE GILL CAFE

A M B L E S I D E

*H*igh
**Sweden Bridge
is on an old
packhorse
route, once a
main highway
from Ambleside
to Hartsop and
Patterdale.**

DISTANCE: 4
miles (6.5km)
TIME: 2½-3
hours
MAP: OS OL 7
TERRAIN:
Good tracks and
paths
throughout.
Steepish climb
after crossing
High Sweden
Bridge.
PARKING:
Main pay-and-
display at north
end of village.
GR 376047.

Rattle Gill Cafe is named after the
lane on which it stands which, in
turn, was named after the rattling of
the wheels on hand carts that
trundled by, over cobbles. They were
on their way to and from the fulling
mill (where cloth was thickened)
further up the beck. The café is very
functional and has a range where
beech logs are burnt. Walkers and all
their gear, plus well behaved dogs,
are made welcome. The food is
homemade and the cream teas are
good. The cafe is open seven days a
week from March to late October
between 10.30am to 6pm, often later
in high summer. During November
and December it opens only at
weekends and it is closed during
January and February. Traditional
jazz is played as background music.

*Ambleside is popular with holiday
makers and an ideal starting place for
a range of walks. It can be noisy not
only with visitors but also with the
sound of becks. These, before tourism
became Ambleside's main industry,
powered 12 mills, including fulling
and carding mills, a linen mill,
bobbin mills, corn mills and sawmills.*

Leave the main car park by the pedestrian footbridge over a stream, cross the busy road, with care, and continue right. Once over the Stock Ghyll beck, turn left for Rattle Gill. Stroll the narrow alley between the quaint old houses until you emerge from an archway, with the teashop to your right. Across the beck is a restored waterwheel.

Go on and then turn left into North Street. Continue past more delightful cottages and alleyways to join Smithy Brow, where you turn right. After 100 yards take the first left along Sweden Bridge Lane. (Sweden, probably derived from Old Norse words meaning a woodland clearing made by burning.) Bear right at the next junction. Go ahead climbing gently to a T-junction, where you turn left. At the end of the lane, go through a gate to walk the old packhorse route, with a delightful view to your left.

Dawdle the rough track between walls and continue where it leads into woodland, with a steep drop down to the beck, which descends in lively falls. Look for pollarded trees, the wood once used for charcoal and for making bobbins.

After one-and-a-quarter miles along the track, and after

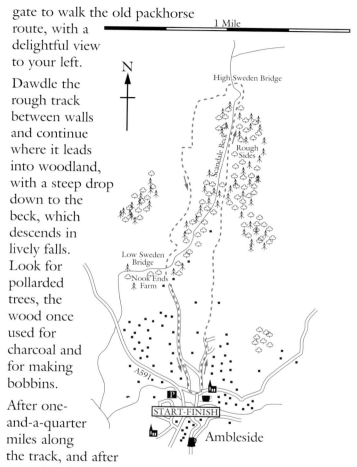

emerging from the trees, you come to High Sweden Bridge, a charming, arched bridge over Scandale Beck with water-worn rocks below. You will want to pause here for your photographs.

Cross the bridge and pass through a gate. Follow the clear path left and follow it as it winds right round a small hillock, easing the gradient. Continue climbing,with the wall to your right, to a ladderstile. Beyond, turn left along the narrow path to a wall where you ascend right to take the next ladderstile, just beyond a sheepfold.

From now on the way is downhill, with Windermere stretched out ahead and the Langdale Pikes, rising above Rydal Water, to your right. The clear, stiled way descends through sheep pastures, with outcrops of rock scattered over the slopes. The path winds round left to cross Low Sweden Bridge, another picturesque crossing of Scandale Beck. Go through the gate and walk on along the pleasing walled Nook Lane, with the spire of the church ahead, piercing the skyline. At the lane end turn left and after a few paces turn right to walk along North Street. The teashop lies a short distance along cobbled Rattle Gill on your right.

CHESTERS

This pleasing walk visits a dramatic force and Loughrigg Tarn. An exciting option is to climb to the summit of Loughrigg Fell.

DISTANCE 6 miles (9.5km) or 7 miles (11km)
TIME: 3-4 hours
MAP: OS OL 7
TERRAIN: Good paths. Steepish climb to Loughrigg Fell.
PARKING: Pay-and-display. GR 341037.

Chesters, named after the owner's dog, stands beside the River Brathay at Skelwith Bridge, between the showroom and the shop of the Kirkstone Galleries. The bridge lies on the A593 between Coniston and Ambleside. If approaching from the latter, turn right just beyond the B5343, the turn for Langdale.

A narrow drive leads to parking outside the teashop. Walkers are invited to park outside while having tea but during the walk they are requested to leave their car in the well signposted National Trust Silverthwaite car park, half-a-mile along the B5343 (Langdale road). Walkers are welcomed, but not dogs. All the food is made on the premises and tea comes in a pot which is large enough for two good-sized cups per person.

The tearoom opens throughout the year except on Christmas and Boxing Day and one week in January. In summer, when the tearoom is open from 10am to 5.30pm, you can take tea on tables outside. In winter it is open from 10am to 5pm. Tel. 015394 32553.

From the car park on the B5343 cross the road and go
through a gap to descend a pitched path. Stride the
footbridge and climb the stile. Walk left to a gate into
deciduous woodland. Stride on along a good path beside
the River Brathay. Here the river hurries on to a narrow
gorge, through which it is forced (Skelwith Force) with
much foaming and noise. There are two viewing
walkways but take care on these if the river is in spate.

Continue on the main path and, after 50 yards, leave it,
left, to join the Langdale Road. Walk on and then cross
to the signposted stile on the opposite side.

Climb steadily through two pastures to a gate towards
the top left corner. This gives access to a glorious tree-
lined path, which leads to Neaum Crag holiday complex.
Clear waymarking takes you steeply uphill, between the
chalets, and where the waymarks cease stroll on ahead

through larch onto the open fell, gained by a step stile.
Ahead magnificent Loughrigg Fell looms over Loughrigg
tarn.

Carry on ahead from the stile, descending a path that
soon becomes a track to a narrow road. Turn left and
walk on to take a stile on the right. Stroll across a
pasture, to the left of the tarn, to a ladderstile. Ignore the
path on the right, which winds round the silvery pool,
and strike up beneath beech, to a gate to a reinforced
track.

Turn left and walk on to a bench seat. Turn right behind
it to take a gate in the fell wall. Turn left and walk on
beside the wall. Ignore a wide gap and continue with the
wall to your left, enjoying the great view ahead. At the
next gate, squeeze through the gap beside it, to come to
a cairn. Here, if you wish to climb to the top of
Loughrigg Fell, turn right and ascend the steep, stony
path. This leads to a grassy trod, still steep, and then the
gradient eases as you approach a T-junction of paths.
Climb left here to reach the summit. From the 1,100 ft
top the view is spectacular and you will want to pause
awhile.

Leave by the cairned way in the direction of Grasmere,
the delightful lake that lies north west. A reinforced path
leads you down to a large, grassy area and then a stone
stairway goes on down and down to Loughrigg Terrace,
where you turn left on the elevated way. Pass through the
gate into woodland. Stride on to join a narrow road,
where you turn right.

If time is short or the weather deteriorates, postpone

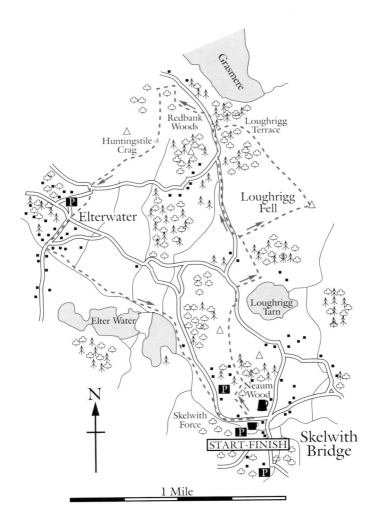

your visit to Loughrigg's summit for another day. At the cairn at the foot of the steep, rough path, go on to climb a stile. Stroll on beneath larch and, beyond the next stile, descend through a meadow to a stile to the narrow road. Turn right and continue to the exit from Loughrigg Terrace and woodland detailed in the paragraph above.

At the brow of the hill ahead take the signposted path on the left. This leads you over fell slopes and into delectable deciduous woodland. Stroll the track to the trees to pass out of the woodland by a kissing gate. Turn left for Elterwater (signposted) and take the left of two gates. This leads you gently uphill and at the brow Elterwater village comes into view in the valley below. Follow one of the paths that descend to the village, crossing a narrow road and then the main road as you go.

Walk into the village and turn left into the car park just before the bridge over the River Brathay. A gate on the right gives access to the path to Skelwith Bridge. The way wanders pleasingly beside the river and then the tarn. Just before the woodland that you entered at the start of the walk, look for the stile on the left, which gives access to the car park. Drive from here for a well earned cup of tea at Chesters.

CONISTON DAIRY

For a good mix of environments, follow this walk as it leads you beside Coniston Water, through glorious oak woodland and back across the wild lower slopes of the Old Man of Coniston.

DISTANCE: 6¹/₂ miles (10.5km)
TIME: 3-4 hours
MAP: OS OL 6
TERRAIN: Generally good walking.
PARKING: In the pay-and-display car park in the centre of Coniston. GR 304976.

Walkers are warmly welcomed at Coniston Dairy. The teashop is open 9am-5.15pm throughout the year and provides a full English tea of sandwiches, scones and a good pot of tea. There are some tables outside. The shop was a dairy for many years and the name was kept for the teashop. All the food is made on the premises. Tel. 01539 541319.

Coniston, frequently busy with tourists, lies tucked between high fells and the lake. It has been the home, temporarily or permanently, of several famous people. These include John Ruskin, the philospher and art critic who lived at Brantwood overlooking the lake, and Beatrix Potter, the writer of children's books and an authority on Herdwick sheep, who owned Monk Coniston estate and eventually bequeathed it to the National Trust.

Turn left out of the car park, noting for your return the teashop across the road. Go by the church, where you might wish to see John Ruskin's

tombstone, a large decorated cross of Coniston stone cut from the Tilberthwaite quarry. Cross the bridge over Church Beck. Continue on, with the garage to your left, and turn left into Lake Road.

Walk on, with John Ruskin School on the right, and then on to the end of the playing fields. Take, on the right, two gates into a pasture. Stride right along the clear path, with the lake away to the left. Go through the next gate and then, at the end of a short hedge, follow a wide track, bearing left across a meadow.

Cross the footbridge over Hagg Beck and continue to a narrow, metalled road, where you swing left. Go on, passing on your left Coniston Hall, a sixteenth century farmhouse with cylindrical chimneys. Stride on along the metalled track, keeping parallel with the lake. On walking

through the campsite, keep to the left branch, heading
for the lakeshore. Stroll the glorious way, right, beside
the water.

Continue on to pass through ancient oak woodland.
Look for the waymark directing you past Torver jetty,
which is used by passengers of the Coniston Launch. Just
beyond, look for another waymark, signposted Torver,
sending you right, away from the lake.

Go on the good track, which leads through a gap in a
wall. Ignore any paths going off right or left. Then carry
on through splendid woodland, where in spring wood
warblers, the nightingales of the north, fill the air with
their lovely songs. Ignore a gate on the right and follow
the distinct way beside a wall on your right. Go through
the next gate, with a dramatic view ahead of Walna Scar,
Dow Crag, the Old Man and Wetherlam.

Walk on beyond the next gate, keeping to the left of
Brackenbarrow Farm, along a track shaded by
magnificent beeches. At the narrow lane, cross, and take
the signposted footpath that points slightly left over a
pasture, to a stile beside the trackbed of the old railway.

*This nine-mile line ran through pleasing countryside. It
once carried large quantities of slate and ore for processing.
Later it carried other goods, tourists, schoolchildren and
many passengers. It was closed in 1958.*

Stroll on ahead to a stile and then keep beside a wall on
your right to join the A593. Turn left, cross the bridge
over Torver Beck and take the right turn, a narrow lane,
with a signpost directing you towards Walna Scar.

Follow the metalled lane as it winds left and right (look

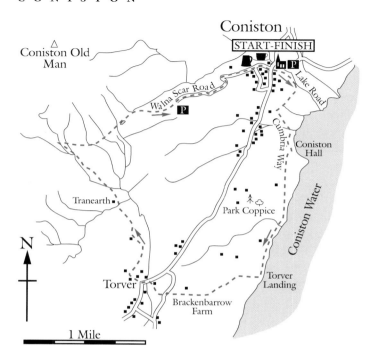

for small signposts directing you along). Carry on where the track ceases to be tarmacked and continue on the walled way, for just over a mile from the A-road, to come to a tractor bridge over the beck, with grand views ahead all the way. Follow the arrows through a series of gates to walk a wide track between two huge spoil heaps.

Wind right round a large quarry hole, where water from the beck descends in a dramatic long plume into the picturesque, flooded Bannishead quarry. Continue upwards on a confusion of paths – the grassy way beside the beck being the most attractive – to come to the very rough track known as Walna Scar Road. In the days of horses and carts, it was a much used way between Coniston and the Duddon valley.

Turn right and keep on the track as it passes along the slopes of the Old Man mountain. Ignore any left or right turns and continue through a small parking area to a gate. Beyond stroll the pleasant, narrow, steeply descending road, all the way to the village. Turn left, cross the bridge over the beck and take the right fork to pass the church and the car park to the cafe just beyond.

THE BLUEBIRD CAFE

C O N I S T O N

A fter a trip on the Gondola, return to Coniston by paths that run high on the fellside.

DISTANCE: 6¹/₂ miles (10 km)
TIME: 3 hours walking after arriving at Parkamoor pier
MAP: OS OL 6
TERRAIN: Generally easy.
PARKING: Free parking behind café on the edge of Coniston Water. GR 308970.

The Bluebird Cafe is open every day, 10am-5pm, from mid-March to the end of the first week in November. Walkers are made very welcome. There are tables on the lake beach for those with dogs. All the food is homemade. The Bluebird Cafe is named after Donald Campbell's car in which he gained the land speed record. He used the same name for the boat in which he broke the water speed record in 1955 and the one in which he was killed when attempting to regain the record in 1967. Cafe Tel. 015394 41649. Gondola sailing times Tel. 015394 41649.

The cafe was built by the Furness Railway Company in 1860 to house the men working on the Gondola. There was a men's messroom and, beyond a partition, the sleeping quarters. The remains of the partition can still be seen in the ceiling. The Gondola was in regular service until 1937, and after that was left to rot away at the southern end of the lake. Forty years later it was rescued and restored by the National Trust and since 1980 has become a familiar sight on the lake.

Turn left off Parkamoor pier onto the lakeside road and walk for 350 yards, making full use of the verge as you proceed along the narrow way. Go right into Dodgson Wood car park and leave by a clear, reinforced track, a permissive path, that winds gently right through fine oak woodland to a National Trust barn.

Keep to the right of the building and follow the way as it continues left behind the barn and beside a wall on your right. Climb the stile, beyond which a board asks you to follow the white arrows and markers. The grand track climbs steadily by gentle zigzags through trees.

After crossing a small stream and following the curving way, don't miss the white waymark and arrow directing you right when the main track turns left. Step across the beck and go on along a narrow path through the wood, waymarked, and with a fence to your left. More arrows direct you left to a stile out of the woodland.

Stroll the narrow, pleasingly sheltered, reinforced track

that continues uphill, with steep slopes to the right and a wall to your left.

The way continues on a grassy path through bracken and joins a wide track that comes in on your right. Turn left and cross the little beck and a stile to climb the slope. Pass in front of Low Parkamoor, a former farmhouse which has been sturdily repaired by the Trust.

Follow the track beyond to pass through a gate and stroll on over moorland, with a dramatic view ahead of Dow Crag. Look right to see Ingleborough and the Howgills. Then the Ill Bell range, Fairfield and Helvellyn come into view.

At the top of the little ridge, the path swings left towards a waymark on a small brow. From here you can see the waterfalls tumbling down the Old Man of Coniston.

Pass through a gate into clear-felled forest, walking a peaty path to emerge onto a forest road, where you bear left. After just half-a-mile, look for the easy-to-miss path going off left, with Scots pine to the right of it and firs to the left. If you reach a junction of forest roads, you have gone too far and need to retrace your steps.

The path soon becomes a wide track, descending through dense conifers at times. It then comes to a large clearing with a splendid view of the lake. To your left is Lawson Park (the experimental station in the book *Plague Dogs*, by Richard Adams). Turn right to walk the track beside the wall – it has a low board directing you on your way.

Go on the good, gated track that steadily descends through woodland and beside walled pastures to join the lakeshore road. Turn left and walk with great care for 300

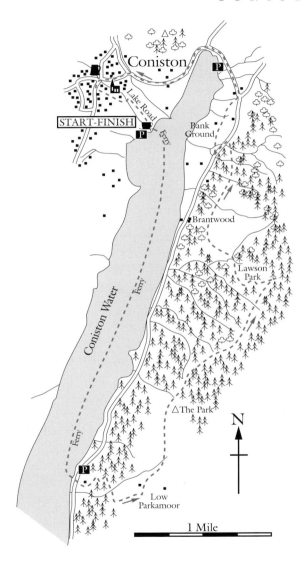

Coniston

Lake Road

START-FINISH

Bank Ground

Brantwood

Lawson Park

Coniston Water

Ferry

△ The Park

N

Low Parkamoor

1 Mile

yards to take the signposted stile on the right. Walk sharp right, parallel with the road you have just traversed, to a kissing gate. Beyond go on with a hedge to your right. Pass through another gate and cross a road, diagonally right, to pass through a third gate on your right.

Stride on to pass Low Bank Ground to your left and then on the gated way to pass High Bank Ground. Just before the ruins of an old tannery, turn left and continue to a stile. Beyond, saunter to a gate. Walk on to the road, where you turn left. Proceed with care, following the road round to the left to pass Monk Coniston car park and go on along the head of the lake.

Cross the road to Hawkshead and take the fenced footpath, walking left in the direction of Coniston. Go on to cross Yewdale Bridge and continue ahead to cross the bridge in the centre of the village. Take the first left turn, following the signpost directions to return to the lakeshore and the Bluebird Cafe.

OLD COBBLERS TEASHOP

T his glorious walk to Tarn Hows takes you over fine pastures, by the beautiful tarn, through quiet woodlands and beside tumbling becks.

DISTANCE:
6¹/₂ miles
(10.5km)
TIME: 3-4
hours
MAP: OS OL 7
TERRAIN: All
tracks and paths
are a pleasure to
walk. Generally
waymarked.
PARKING:
Large car park
on edge of
village – can
become full in
the summer. GR
354981.

The tiny Old Cobblers Teashop stands on one of Hawkshead's fine cobbled lanes. It is named after the building's former use. It opens all year round, excluding Sundays, two weeks in November and one in March. It serves from 10am to 4.15pm in winter and for half an hour extra in summer. It makes walkers and their muddy boots most welcome. Even small, well behaved dogs can sit under the tea table while you enjoy the delicious home-made fare. As all the teashops in Hawkshead close on a different day, perhaps on a Sunday you could round off your walk at Grandy Nook, or the Minstrels Gallery, both enjoyable teashops. Tel. 015394 36707 (Old Cobblers).

Before the 12th century Hawkshead was an area of swamp and tangled woodland. In 1578 Hawkshead became a parish. William Wordsworth attended the Grammar School, which was founded in 1585. Until as late as the early 1800s the few roads were fit only for those on foot or horseback. Today Hawkshead attracts large numbers of tourists and yet, because of

good traffic management and a well placed car park, still manages to retain the charm of a small village from another age. Its narrow cobbled streets, archways, snug stone cottages and crooked lanes seem quite unchanged from Wordsworth's day or that of Beatrix Potter, who also was a devotee of its quaintness.

Turn left out of the car park and walk towards the church. Bear right to walk through the virtually traffic-free streets to go left up Vicarage Lane. Continue along the narrow way to pass Ann Tyson's Cottage, where Wordsworth lodged while at school.

Turn right onto the waymarked footpath to Tarn Hows. Go on beside the fence on your right to climb to a kissing gate ahead, enjoying the good views as you dawdle. Stride on the clear, gated way to pass a pretty gill with a dancing beck on your right. The path crosses the stream on a tractor bridge and then carries on its winding way to a stile.

Beyond, follow the path, to go over an access track and then bear gently right to a kissing gate in the far right corner to join a busy road. Turn left and walk with care through the hamlet of Hawkshead Hill, passing, on the right, the Baptist Chapel built in 1678.

Take the next right turn for Tarn Hows to walk a quiet lane. At a small triangle of roads, in front of a large white house named Summerhill, keep right. Walk on to take the signposted track on the left and follow it through the tiny cluster of houses at Bettyfold. Go through a gate and continue on a walled track which leads towards larch woodland.

Beyond the next gate you enter pastures. Once through a further gate, walk ahead to cross a meeting of tracks. Take the fine stile, with its dog gate, on your right and then walk ahead, with a walled woodland to your right and opening pastures to your left. Follow the narrow path as it curves left towards Rose Castle, a delightful, tiny house belonging to the National Trust, which you pass on its right side.

A good track curves steadily left and brings you to a bird's-eye view of the delectable Tarn Hows. Walk left to a signpost, where you turn right and then left to continue

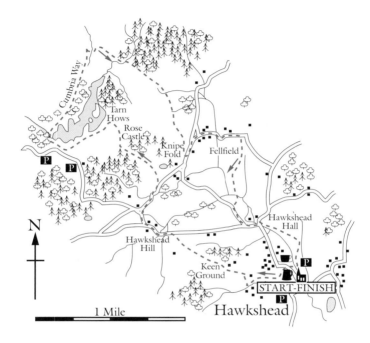

in a clockwise direction around, and closer to, the lovely stretch of water. Here are well placed seats for picnics from where you can watch the many birds attracted by the tarn.

Continue on to pass through a gate and 50 yards on take a good track right to continue around the pool. Press on the good path, now proceeding along the opposite bank to the one by which you approached the tarn. Enjoy the lovely way until you reach a three-armed signpost. Here turn left to walk in the direction of Arnside and the Langdales, the track taking you through more open ground with scattered birch and much bracken.

After stepping over a low ladderstile, turn right to climb the reinforced track, an old packhorse route, where you can delight in walking where many, over the ages, have passed before. You feel that at any moment you will meet with a train of ponies.

At the brow of the hill, look right for another glimpse of the picturesque tarn. Ahead you can see Hawkshead and Esthwaite Water and to the left stretches Windermere. The pleasing track goes on and on and then steadily begins to descend to the road. Turn left and, after Borwick Fold Farm, take an even narrower lane on the right.

This passes through the tiny hamlet of Knipe Fold. Just before a cottage on the right, Ben Fold, turn right to walk a hedged track. Go through a kissing gate and follow a waymarked, rutted track to a stile, with a dog gate, in the far right corner. Beyond, walk ahead over a pasture to cross a stream by a huge slab of slate and then bear diagonally towards buildings on your right, to join a narrow lane.

Turn left and continue to the B5285. Turn left again and walk with care past the woodyard to the B5286. Cross and, slightly to the left, pass through a huge, signposted, iron gate with a heavy catch. Walk beside Black Beck, where you should see at least one pair of dippers. Continue to the footbridge, which you cross. Stride the track, past Black Beck cottage, to the main road.

Cross and walk ahead through a cobbled yard and under an arch to turn right to take tea at the Old Cobblers.

THE FOREST TEAROOM

T his is a good walk for any time of the year.

DISTANCE: 3 miles (5km) or 5¹/₂ miles (9km)
TIME: 1¹/₂ hours or 3 hours
MAP: OS OL 7
TERRAIN: Easy walking on forest roads. Some paths are rough underfoot. The shorter walk is waymarked. The longer walk leaves Carron Crag and uses rights-of-way which are not signposted. Map reading helpful.
PARKING: Visitor Centre. GR 336944.

The tearoom, a pleasing, airy room with a pine floor, was once a garage. It is open seven days a week except from New Year until early February. Meals are served between 10am and 4pm in winter and for an hour longer in the summer. All the food is made on the premises. Walkers, including their boots, rucksacks and waterproofs, are warmly welcomed. Dogs must be left outside. There are picnic tables in the courtyard. Tel. 01229 860011.

Grizedale Hall was demolished after the 1939-45 war. It had housed German prisoners of war. Across the road from the site, the outbuildings of the old hall have been converted into a visitor centre. Annually 350,000 visitors are attracted to Grizedale, many for the arts programmes and many to walk. With 8,700 acres of woodland to explore, you can walk for miles using the well maintained paths, tracks and forest roads and meet only a handful of other people.

From the forest shop walk towards

the children's attractive play area and then turn left to pass through a large, green door in a high wall. Turn right and follow the trail marker posts banded with red. Walk the metalled lane to pass Home Farm and then bear slightly right and then left to climb a steep track, signposted Coniston.

Continue up and up until you reach a forest road. Turn right. After 200 yards take a left turn, banded with red and pale green bands, to ascend a rough path that climbs steadily through the plantations. Pause by some old gate stoops to look down on the dale below and the glorious ridge of the Ill Bell range.

Three-quarters of a mile from the start of the path, look for the red and green banded posts directing you left through larch. After 150 yards turn left to stride a forest road. Ignore all side turns and walk on to where the road

curves sharply left. Here, go through the gate in a deer
fence on your right. Climb steadily following the
waymarking up through young trees and heather until
you reach Carron Crag (1,025 feet/314m). Scramble up
the side of the tiny summit to enjoy a breathtaking 360-
degrees view.

*You are now at the highest point of the forest and from it
you can see the Lakeland fells, the Howgills, the Yorkshire
hills and the waters of Morecambe Bay.*

Go on to descend from the crag and follow the marker
posts down through the young trees to another deer gate.
Beyond, turn right to come, in a few yards, to a junction
of tracks. Here a decision has to be made, either to
return to the visitor centre or to continue on the longer
walk.

To return, bear sharp left. Descend the way to a forest
road. Cross and go down the steep track taken at the
outset of your walk. At the road, walk on past the farm.
Don't miss the green door in the wall on the left to reach
the visitor centre.

To extend the walk, turn right at the cross of tracks and
paths, to stroll a wide forest road. At the next junction of
roads and paths, walk straight ahead climbing a pleasing,
rougher track through trees into a much wilder area of
the forest.

This track brings you to another forest road, where you
turn left. As you go look for the tiny white houses of the
village of Satterthwaite in the valley far below. It is at this
point that you leave the continuing road to take one
going off right. This leads you over a concrete bridge

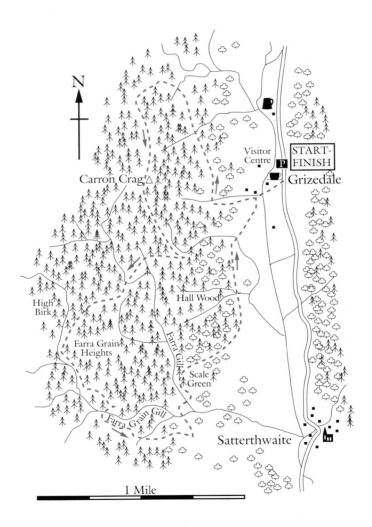

N

Carron Crag △

Visitor Centre

START-FINISH

Grizedale

High Birk

Farra Grain Heights

Farra Gill

Hall Wood

Scale Green

Farra Grain Gill

Satterthwaite

1 Mile

above Farra Grain Gill, with the stream tumbling noisily downhill over its rocky bed of Silurian slate.

Climb the slope beyond and go on beside an area of new planting with a deer fence, to your left. Where the fence turns left (350 yards from the bridge), you do the same to descend an easy-to-miss pleasant track with grass growing down its middle. (The track drops left just before a 'no cycling' sign.) Go down and down to join a forest road and turn left.

Keep on this way as it curves downhill to a delightful hollow with picnic tables and a stone bridge over the beck crossed earlier. Before you walk on over the bridge and carry on along the green banded trail through trees, walk upstream to see one of Grizedale's famous collection of carvings and artefacts. This is a beautifully carved overshot waterwheel complete with its own small leat.

Saunter through the trees to cross another stone bridge over a second beck, with Farra Grain Lower Bridge carved on its parapet. You then rejoin the road. and go on right. As you dawdle on look for more structures among the trees. Remain on the road, ignoring the green banded posts as they go off left.

Enjoy striding the road as it passes beside deciduous woodland, with glorious pastures away to the right. At a Y-junction, take the right branch that leads to a cattle grid and a gate into a large field. Stroll the track which brings you back to Home Farm. Turn right to walk on to take the gate in the wall, hopefully in time for tea.

BUCKLE YEAT TEASHOP

NEAR SAWREY

This delightful walk takes you along a quiet reach of Lake Windermere. You may wish to end your day with a visit to Beatrix Potter's farm, Hill Top.

DISTANCE: 6 miles (10km)
TIME: 3 hours
MAP: OS OL 7
TERRAIN: Generally easy walking. A short steady climb into Garnett Wood.
PARKING: A few vehicles can be parked at the side of the cottage. GR 370956.

The name Buckle Yeat means 'fasten the gate'. The charming cottage, which is almost next door to Hill Top, features in Beatrix Potter's *Tale of Tom Kitten*. It opens to coincide with the opening times of Hill Top – that is, Easter to the end of October, 10am-4.30pm, closed on Thursdays and Fridays. Walkers receive a great welcome in the oak-beamed dining room, with its large, leaded grate. Dogs, and their owners, can take tea in the pretty gardens behind the cottage. All the goodies are homemade. Tel. 015394 36446.

Sawrey is made up of Far and Near Sawrey. Hill Top at Near Sawrey is owned by the National Trust, which maintains it much as it was in Beatrix's day. The Tower Bank Arms stands next to Buckle Yeat and it too features in the famous stories. The church of St Peter is described by Nikolaus Pevsner as "a decent, honest piece of work".

Turn right out of Buckle Yeat to pass the Tower Bank Arms and then Hill

Top. At the brow, just beyond, take the footpath, signposted 'To the Ferry', on the right. The well made path, fenced on the right and walled to the left, descends gently and delightfully to a clapper bridge. Follow the signposted, reinforced path diagonally across a meadow, in the direction of the church, to a kissing gate. Beyond turn left.

The narrow lane passes Fold Farm, which has a 1700 datestone. At the three-armed signpost, by the Y-junction, take the right branch to walk on towards the Sawrey Hotel, where you cross the road. Go right to take, now on your left, the public footpath, a wide hedged track, to 'The Ferry'.

Continue, climbing steadily, to a tall, metal kissing gate in the right corner of the track. Go on past Sawrey Knotts, from where there is a glimpse of Lake Windermere. Carry on to another similar kissing gate.

Beyond, descend the track to cross an access lane and to continue downhill to the main road.

Cross the road and descend, with care, to pass Fair Rigg and to pick up another signposted footpath beyond the wall. At the end of this stretch, remain on the road for a hundred yards to take a wide track, on your right.

Dawdle the pleasing way close to the edge of the lake. When the track becomes metalled and turns inland, follow it to its end to join a road. Turn left to walk through woodland for 650 yards to a point where the road turns sharp right. Here go ahead over a signposted stile, bear left and continue beside the lake. Enjoy this glorious path, which in summer is lined with wild flowers and where there are many birds to be seen.

As you near a gate, close to the water's edge, look for the much photographed Ling Holme island. Pass two boathouses to stroll on along a clear track through a copse, where in spring kingcups, violets, milkmaids and wood anemones flower in profusion.

Cross a bridge over a deepish beck entering the lake and then go on where the water almost laps the path. Press on over duck boards and then climb a stone stepped stile into Rawlinson Nab. Stroll on the delightful path below oaks and beside the lake. Continue on and then finally follow the way inland along a narrow path to a ladderstile to a quiet road.

Turn right to pass below deciduous trees and walk to (on the right) Low Cunsey Farm. Opposite, take a wide track through conifers. Remain on the main track and at the waymark bear left, with a small stream, through bushes,

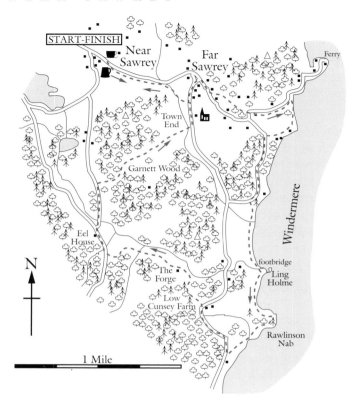

to your right. Pass the derelict forge and walk ahead to the end of the track. The way goes on as a footpath, with deer fencing to the left.

Follow the way (which can be very muddy after a wet winter) all the way to a road. Go right and walk on to a cottage on the right, beyond which you turn right again. Walk the gently climbing lane. Pass the toad crossing sign and just beyond take the footpath on the right. It climbs steadily into deciduous woodland. Follow the waymarked way, up and up until the lovely path brings you to a stile, beyond which you emerge from the trees in park-like pastures.

Walk ahead. Ignore the track that swings left and saunter on to an easy-to-miss stile. Go through the next gate and then veer slightly left to go ahead beside a fenced copse. Climb the next stile and then stride the clear, terraced, grassy path to a lane. Bear left to pass a row of cottages.

The entrance to the church is on the right. It was built in 1869 to seat as many as 400 people; many fine houses were being built at this time and all the servants were expected to attend services with their employers.

Leave the church by the same gate and walk on to the end of the cottages in the lane, to take the kissing gate, on the left, from which you emerged early in the walk. Take the signposted footpath to return to Buckle Yeat.

BOOTH'S TEASHOP

W I N D E R M E R E

This walk takes you through pleasing, park-like pastures above Windermere.

DISTANCE: 5 miles (8km)
TIME: 3 hours
MAP: OS OL 7
TERRAIN: Good paths and tracks, all generally well waymarked. A little gentle climbing.
PARKING: In front of Windermere Station, where you can park all day for a reasonable sum. GR 414987.

Booth's teashop is situated in the old waiting room of Windermere Station, where the high ceilings and mouldings have been retained. It has a fine stained-glass window taken from Booth's teashop in Southport. Although it adjoins the busy supermarket, to which it belongs, it has a pleasant, relaxed atmosphere and you may be tempted to take tea in the sunny conservatory extension which projects into the station yard. It opens all year except for Sundays, Bank Holidays, Christmas Day and Boxing Day, from 9am to 4.30pm. Walkers are welcome and there is space for their rucksacks and waterproofs. No dogs are allowed and the teashop has a no smoking policy.

In 1847 the railway came to the village of Windermere, at that time just a scattering of hamlets and farms. From then on the area became attractive to the businessmen of Manchester. They built large houses surrounded by delightful parkland and from these they could commute daily. Today housing estates cover much of the parkland but just beyond

there remain glorious meadows and fell slopes, and this walk takes you among them.

Continue east out of the station yard to walk through the car park of Lakeland Limited (once Lakeland Plastics). Note the time when the gates to this second car park are closed – this is not a right of way but the firm allows its use, so saving pedestrians some walking along the busy A591.

Turn left to walk up Thwaites Lane and then right for 100 yards along the A-road. Take the signposted gate on the right just beyond the farm. Walk ahead to climb the stile over a fence and then on to pass through a gate. Beyond, bear slightly left to cross a pasture to a kissing gate and then on to another. Still bearing left, take the stile that gives access to a path leading to the railway line.

Cross with care and descend to pass between garages. Bear left and go ahead, crossing roads where they swing left or right. Continue, in the same direction, along a lane to go over a small stone bridge. Turn right at the signpost and stroll the pleasant way to pass through a kissing gate.

Turn left and climb uphill, keeping parallel with the wall on your left, to pass through a kissing gate in the wall at the top of the pasture (this is the gate you return to on the way back). Follow the short, pitched path just beyond the gate and climb steadily to the top of School Knott, a pleasing knoll with a spectacular view. Below lies School Knott tarn.

Descend to the tarn and bear round right, keeping the pretty pool to your left. Stroll on to a kissing gate through the wall on your left, under four tall conifers, to join the Dales Way. Once through the gate bear left, uphill, to the top left corner to pass through a gap in the wall. Walk ahead to the next waymark and turn left to stroll the quiet valley, between slopes, to a stile to Hag End Farm.

Go ahead, keeping left of the barns and then right of the farmhouse to walk the access track to a narrow road. Go left here and after 200 yards take the signposted footpath across a pasture on your left. Climb the stile, turn right and walk beside the fence to the next stile. Then drop down a slope to a narrow road.

Cross and take the stile over a double row of fencing and continue beside the fence of Yews, an attractive dwelling on your right. Negotiate more fencing, go over the access track and more fencing to bear right to a ladderstile over the wall on your right. Beyond continue through

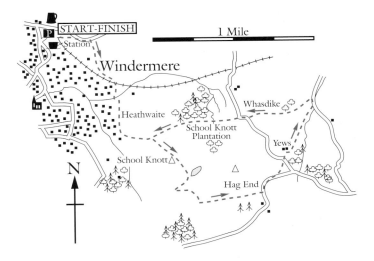

scattered oaks and drop down to a gate in the bottom left corner.

Bear slightly left to stride a tractor bridge over a small ditch and head on for the far right corner, at the side of another small stream. Climb the stile over the fence and go over the mire on stepping stones. Walk on to join the gated road to Ings.

After a 100 yards, head left along a signposted path that gradually moves away from the wall on your right to a gate into Whasdike Wood, which is particularly lovely in spring. Emerge from the woodland and go on to join a metalled road, where you turn left. Continue ahead to go through a gate and, just beyond and where the road swings sharp right, go ahead as directed by the signpost.

Head for the small, corrugated-roofed barn, with its

prominent waymark and then climb a mound, similarly waymarked. The path then continues to a step stile into School Knott Plantation. Stride ahead through trees and onto open ground. Watch out for a faint branching of the way. The left branch takes you along the skirt of School Knott, climbed earlier. If you miss this and find yourself following tractor tracks, go on ahead with the wall well away to the right. Ignore the next two gates through the wall and continue until you come to the kissing gate, in the wall on your right, taken earlier.

Go through the gate and retrace your outward route.

This walk takes you through Eskdale's verdant woodlands and pastures to the craggy grandeur about the Roman fort. It returns along pleasing paths, keeping in sight and sound of the River Esk.

DISTANCE:
6¹/₂ miles/10km
TIME: 4 hours
MAP: OS OL 6
TERRAIN:
Easy walking.
PARKING:
Dalegarth
Station. GR
174007.

Brook House lies 200 yards east of the car park. It serves delightful cream teas in the hotel or outside in an extensive drystone walled enclosure. It has two specialities: one, the very warm welcome given to all comers by the owners and, two, the magnificent murals on the walls of the toilets! Walkers and their boots, and dogs, are particularly welcome, both indoors and outside. Brook House is open all day, every day. Tel. 019467 23288.

Eskdale has a network of old roads, some of which have been metalled while others remain as delightful footpaths and tracks. The dale has many fine waterfalls which tumble down craggy slopes and through wooded ravines. St Catherine's Church, Boot, lies hidden away at the end of an old lane and close to a wide sweep of the River Esk.

It was built of local stone in the 17th century. Standing in the churchyard is the fine granite gravestone of Tommy Dobson, a Master of Foxhounds, who died at the age of 83 while hunting in Langdale.

Turn left out of the car park to walk the narrow lane to come to Brook House. Then take the signposted byway that goes off right, opposite. Follow this to come to St Catherine's Church, which you may like to visit. At the edge of the river, turn left and walk on to a division of the track. Here take the right fork to continue beside the cascading, turquoise Esk.

The path leads to a fine, gated bridge over a gorge through which the river, now green, surges. Look for the girders on which the bridge rests.

These once supported an earlier bridge which carried the mineral railway from the mines on the far bank to Dalegarth. The present bridge was built in 1990 in memory of Geoffrey Berry, former secretary of Friends of the Lake District.

Once across walk straight ahead along a narrow, indistinct path below trees to join a wide track, where you turn left. Leave the woodland by a gate and then

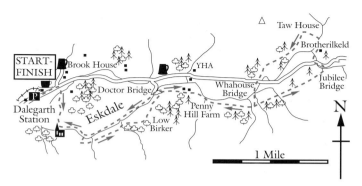

step out along a grassy path that continues through the valley, with extensive views ahead of Crinkle Crags and Bowfell.

Pass through a gate and cross the footbridge over Birker Beck, foaming white as it makes its angry way to join the Esk. Go on along the way and, where the path divides, keep to the left fork to pass in front of Low Birker cottage. Carry on along the wide track to the charming Doctor Bridge – but do not cross.

Walk the hedged lane to pass in front of Penny Hill Farm (once an inn). This is one of the farms bought by Beatrix Potter for the National Trust. The clear path continues idyllically on through pastures, fords Spothow Gill and comes to a three-armed signpost. (This is where you retrace your steps on part of the return route.) Look for the footbridge over Dodknott Gill and then pass through delightful woodland. Emerge from the trees onto a high path on open fell below towering Harter Fell. As you continue you can see the narrow road climbing up Hardknott Pass.

115

BROOK HOUSE

E S K D A L E

Look ahead to see the outline of the Roman fort below rugged Hard Knott. The path slopes gently downwards and then passes through two kissing gates. Descend to the little stone Jubilee Bridge over Hardknott Beck. If you wish to visit the fort, turn right and climb the pass. To continue the walk, turn left and descend to the signposted track, on the right, to Brotherilkeld Farm, which has been owned by the National Trust since 1961. Continue on the footpath beside the beck, with the farm to your right, to cross the fine wooden footbridge over the River Esk.

Walk ahead along a fenced track to come to Taw House Farm. Go through the gate and walk left, to begin your return, passing behind the farmhouse. Stride the access track and press on through the dale. Turn left beyond the last wall before the track reaches the road through the valley.

Drop down the slope, turn left to cross the fine Whahouse Bridge and take the signposted footpath on the right. Saunter across the meadow to go over a footbridge and follow the arrowed path to a gate into deciduous woodland. Follow the path up through the trees to the three-armed signpost once again.

Turn right and retrace your outward route to Doctor Bridge, which you cross. Stroll left and walk the distinct path beside the Esk and continue where it passes through bracken high above the surging river. As you progress through a walled track, look across the valley to see the white tresses of Birker Force. The track returns to St Catherine's church. A right turn brings you back to the road and Brook House.

BROUGHTON TEASHOP

This country walk takes you into the remote Lickle Valley. The river, in places petulant, flows through this gentle, secret corner of Cumbria and accompanies you for much of the walk.

DISTANCE: 6 miles (10km)
TIME: 3 hours
MAPS: OS OL 6 (new series)
TERRAIN: Easy walking.
PARKING: In Broughton Square. GR 212875.

For many years there has been a small cafe behind the counter of Broughton Bakery. In April 1998, under the new ownership of a local family, the shop was extended and now the teashop takes up the full length of the building, with bread and cakes sold in a smaller area to one side. The building dates back to the early 1700s when it is thought to have been a farmhouse, but it has been a bakery for 70 years. Traditionally the cafe has been a meeting place for farmers, on regular sale days at Broughton Auction Mart. A warm welcome is offered to walkers. It is open all year, except Sundays, Christmas Day and Boxing Day, from 9am to 5pm (2pm on Wednesdays). Tel 01229 716284.

Broughton has a population of about 1,000. It lies close to the River Duddon, which starts life as a mountain stream and in its lower reaches opens into a broad, sandy estuary. The village stands on the southern side of a gentle hill. It has held a market charter, granted by Henry III, since 1245. Once the chief occupation of the villagers was making hoops, baskets (known locally as swills), brushstocks, and shafts for rakes and forks. Thirteen craftsmen worked with coppiced wood from the Furness fells. Today, the lovely square is surrounded by town houses built in Georgian times. Horse chestnuts, glorious in blossom and magnetic to the young in conker time, shade stocks, fish slabs and an obelisk erected for George III's jubilee in 1810.

Turn left out of the teashop and then walk right up Griffin Street to enter the square. Leave it by the first left turn to walk New Street (constructed around 1792). Remain on the left side of the road as you round the blind corner and continue for 100 yards to take the signposted gate on the right.

Stride ahead across the pasture to a ladderstile over the far boundary fence. Turn left to walk a track and then leave it, right, just before a gate to the road. Continue right, with a wall and a tiny stream to the left. Near the top left corner, step across the stream to a stile. It gives direct access to the busy Coniston road, so proceed with care.

Go through the gap stile opposite and stroll on, right, through four stiles. The next stile also lies directly ahead across a pasture that is frequently muddy. Once over the stile, turn left and pass the farmhouse to take, on your right, a footbridge over Hagg Beck. Go on ahead, gradually moving up the slope to a small copse and then descend to a stile. Pass below a glorious ash to stride a

green trod to a gap stile beside a gate. Beyond, a hidden walled track leads you round left to a stile and then to another onto a narrow road.

Turn right and, after a few yards, pass through a gate on the left and walk on along a pasture high above the River Lickle. Pause here to enjoy this delightful valley and the view of Stickle Pike and Caw. Continue on the stiled way, crossing two small streams and then head towards a small arched way between barns.

Pass the fine dwelling of Lumholme to join a good track along which you can stride out. Pass a cottage, once a bobbin mill, and go on to walk between cottages known as Shuttle Street, where weavers once lived. Continue to the road. You are now in the hamlet of Broughton Mills.

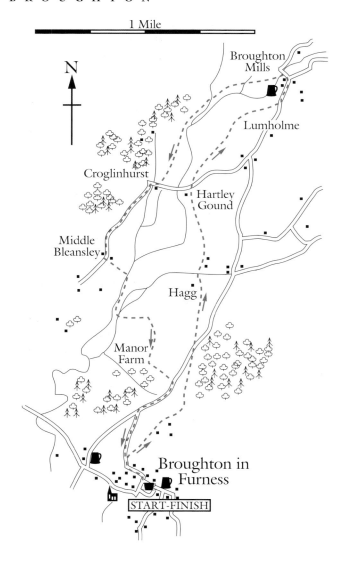

Turn left and pass the Blacksmith's Arms (1748). Drop down the hill to pass a converted corn mill. Cross the river by the fine stone bridge and take the signposted footpath on the left.

Head towards the copse and, once through it, bear right to walk a pasture and then beside a fence to a gap stile in the wall. Beyond, stride ahead across another pasture to pass through a wall gap. Stroll left, with the Lickle, descending in lively falls, close on your left. Climb the ladderstile and beyond bear half right to cross a shallow feeder stream. Go on through a gate beside the Lickle and climb the next stone-stepped stile. Go through another gate and then on to a step stile to the narrow road. Turn right and follow it as it swings left.

Saunter this pleasing way to take the signposted path on the left, opposite Middle Bleansley cottage. This leads you down to the Lickle once more. Cross the wide tractor bridge and turn right to walk the permissive path, with the beck to your right. At the next bridge turn left, away from the river, to follow a raised track to a stile in the boundary hedge. Turn right and continue steadily uphill to pass Manor Farm and on to the A593 – the road from Broughton to Coniston.

Turn right and walk into Broughton and the teashop.

THE PEPPERMILL

他his walk follows a canal, continues beside an estuary and visits a fine stone circle.

DISTANCE: 8½ miles (14km)
TIME: 4 hours
MAPS: OS OL 6 (new series) and Pathfinder 636 37/47
TERRAIN: Pleasing paths and tracks. Some unavoidable road and shingle shore walking.
PARKING: Brewery pay-and-display, overlooking the A590. GR 288784.

The Peppermill stands tucked away on the south end of cobbled Market Street, a hundred yards from the car park. It is a busy restaurant and all are made welcome. The narrow shop frontage belies the depth of the shop and at the back of the building lies a charming walled garden edged with bushes and flowers. Climb stone steps to tables, which stand on ascending terraces. They are very popular in summer, and walkers can take their dogs. The food is made on the premises. It is open all the year from 9am onwards, except for Sundays. Tel. 01229 587564.

Ulverston has a small, friendly market, which on busy days almost reaches The Peppermill. Once the town had many mills producing bobbins, malt, hoops, canvas, linen-check and sailcloth. Other products, including slate, bar-iron, iron-ore and gunpowder, needed to be exported by sea and in 1796 the town was linked with the Leven Estuary by a mile-long canal, engineered by John Rennie. A triangle of trade developed: gunpowder was exported to Africa, where it was exchanged for slaves who

were taken to work in the plantations of America. Raw cotton was brought back to Ulverston's new spinning mills.

Leave the car park and, remaining on the same side of the road, head away (east) from the town.

The three-storey houses in the fine terrace to your left were once occupied by the families of ships' captains who sailed out of the canal basin. Above, on Hoad Hill, stands a tall monument, an imitation of the Eddystone lighthouse, to Sir John Barrow, under-secretary to the Admiralty and Ulverston's famous son.

Remain on the noisy A590 to the end of the protective railings to come level with the far end of the Canal Tavern. Cross and walk down beside the inn to stroll alongside the canal.

This lovely, quiet stretch of water, where only ducks, gulls and swans disturb its placid surface, has meadows on one side. Towards its end, on the opposite bank, stands the huge GlaxoWellcome plant. What a change of sight and sound from when innumerable boats travelled to and from Ulverston's factories lining the canal.

At the derelict lock gates and the bridge over the end of the canal (plugged in 1949), look left to see the dramatic Leven railway viaduct, strung across the waters of the estuary. The railway brought a decline in trade on the canal and finally its demise. Cross the canal and then walk right, following the Cumbria Way (CW) sign to pass the Bay Horse restaurant. Continue for three-quarters of a mile, inland, beside the Glaxo factory, now on your right.

Turn left, along the CW, and head towards the Sea View Inn (today, a long way from the shore). Go right and then bear left, in the direction of Sandhall, to walk a hedged lane. Cross Carter Beck and take the waymarked (CW) kissing gate on the left and walk diagonally across a pasture, in the direction of a huge slag-heap, to a stile.

Beyond, stride a wide, gated track to pass near to a tall, brick chimney which stands forlorn and alone and where once bricks were made.

Beyond, rearing above the treetops, stands Conishead Priory, the home of the Braddyll family in the mid 17th

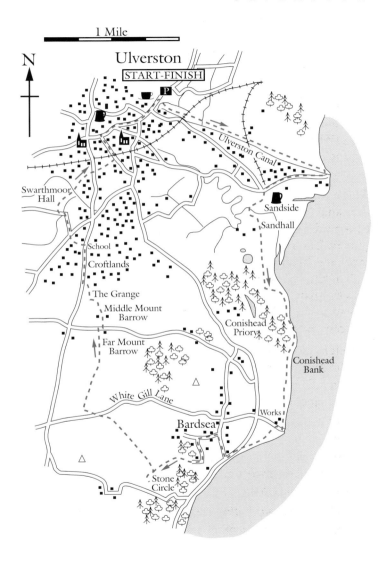

century. It was rebuilt by 1836. Today it is a Buddhist centre. Look right to see a hermitage on a hill. This was built by Colonel Braddyll to house a hermit who was paid to live there.

Join a hedged lane and follow it as it swings left to the side of the estuary. Turn right to walk a hedged way and then the shingle shore.

Out in the calm waters stands Chapel Island, its few trees framing the remnants of another folly built by the colonel. This island provided a half-way refuge for travellers to Ulverston on the treacherous route across the sands. Those who crossed the sands over the centuries included the Roman armies, Robert the Bruce, George Fox, John Wesley and William Wordsworth.

Continue along the shoreline for nearly two miles to a small parking area by an industrial unit. Turn right for 100 yards and then take a bridleway on the left to cut off a large breech in the shallow cliffs. The track returns you to the shoreline below the charming village of Bardsea, where there are picnic tables, toilets and a cafe.

Cross the busy coast road and climb a narrow lane, to the right of the toilet block. Turn left beyond the Braddyll Arms and follow a lane out into the lovely countryside. At the T-junction, stroll left to pass through the tiny hamlet of Wellhouse. When the metalled road ceases, continue on the ascending reinforced track in the direction of Birkrigg Common.

Enjoy this delightful way, which provides ever-increasing views of the estuary and the village and has a glorious bluebell wood to the right.

Go through the gate onto the common and take the first grassy swathe to the left to see the Bronze Age stone circle. Ten stones stand short but proud around what might have been a place of cremation. The view is stupendous. Return to the gate. Do not pass through but follow the wall on your right to the brow of the common, where a grand view of the Lakeland mountains awaits.

At the wall corner follow one of several grassy swathes, bearing steadily left through the bracken and descending towards White Gill Lane. Hopefully you have arrived at a three-armed signpost (grid ref. 284748). Cross the lane and follow the footpath sign directing you towards a stile into a fine wide walled track. At Red Lane, turn right and, after 20 yards, turn left into the access track to Middle Mount Barrow Farm.

Go through the gate, bear slightly right to stride a metalled track. Ignore a right turn and follow the lane as it bears left. Just before the first house on the right, take the easy-to-miss gate on the right. Walk the gated way to a road. Walk on and then bear left in front of The Lancastrian pub. Walk right along Mountbarrow Road and, when opposite the primary school, turn left into Meeting House Lane to pass the Quaker meeting house. Cross Urswick Road and continue down Swarthmoor Hall Lane to the Hall.

The fine Elizabethan house, built by Judge Fell (the first husband of Margaret Fox, who later married George Fox, the Quaker leader), dates from the 16th century. The three-storey building is open mid March to mid October, on Mondays, Tuesdays, Wednesdays and Saturdays.

U L V E R S T O N

Just beyond the house walk the unsignposted cart track on the right. Follow the clear, gated path through a meadow and over a beck to come to Springfield Road. Cross and walk left and then right along Conishead Road. Pass left under the railway bridge and continue ahead to the A590. Cross and walk right. The first left leads to The Peppermill in Market Street. The car park lies to the right at the start of the cobbled way.